REVISE EDEXCEL GCSE (9–1)
Biology

REVISION WORKBOOK

Foundation

Series Consultant: Harry Smith
Author: Dr Stephen Hoare

For the full range of Pearson revision titles across KS2, KS3, GCSE, Functional Skills, AS/A Level and BTEC visit:
www.pearsonschools.co.uk/revise

Contents

A small bit of small print:
Edexcel publishes Sample Assessment Material and the Specification on its website. This is the official content and this book should be used in conjunction with it. The questions have been written to help you practice every topic in the book. Remember: the real exam questions may not look like this.

Plant and animal cells

1 (a) Which of the following are found in both animal and plant cells?

   ☐ **A** cell membrane, nucleus, chloroplast

   ☐ **B** cell membrane, nucleus, ribosomes

   ☐ **C** cell wall, nucleus, ribosomes

   ☐ **D** cell wall, mitochondria, ribosomes

> Look at the mark allocation for each question – here there is one mark so you need to put a cross in **one** box.

(1 mark)

(b) Which of the following are found only in plant cells?

   ☐ **A** cell membrane, nucleus, chloroplast

   ☐ **B** cell membrane, vacuole, chloroplast

   ☐ **C** cell wall, chloroplast, vacuole

   ☐ **D** cytoplasm, chloroplast, vacuole

> Always answer multiple-choice questions, even if you don't actually know the answer.

(1 mark)

2 (a) Describe the function of mitochondria.

....

....

.... **(2 marks)**

(b) Explain why all plant cells contain mitochondria but only some contain chloroplasts.

> Chloroplasts need light to carry out photosynthesis. Use the function of a chloroplast to explain why you would not find them in certain cells, such as root cells.

....

....

....

.... **(2 marks)**

3 Describe the difference between the functions of a cell membrane and a cell wall.

Guided

Cell membrane controls ....

....

....

.... **(2 marks)**

4 Enzymes are proteins made in cells. Pancreatic cells produce large amounts of enzymes but fat cells do not. Suggest an explanation for why pancreatic cells contain many more ribosomes than fat cells.

....

....

....

.... **(2 marks)**

Different kinds of cell

1 The genes in a bacterial cell are contained:

☐ **A** on a circular chromosome only

☐ **B** on plasmids only

☐ **C** on plasmids and a circular chromosome

☐ **D** ~~in the nucleus~~   It cannot be D because bacteria do not have nuclei.   **(1 mark)**

2 The diagram shows a sperm cell and a bacterium. Note that the drawings are not to the same scale.

A

B

Sperm cell   Bacterium

(a) Name the structures labelled A and B in the diagram:

A ....

B .... **(2 marks)**

(b) Describe the function of each structure.

A ....

....

B ....

.... **(2 marks)**

3 Breathing can expose us to dust, dirt and bacteria.

Explain how cells in the lungs are specialised to protect us from these.

....

....

....

....

....

.... **(3 marks)**

Microscopes and magnification

1 Scientists use two types of microscope to examine cells: light microscopes and electron microscopes. Describe how these types of microscope are different.

Light microscopes magnify .... than electron microscopes.

The level of cell detail seen with an electron microscope is ....

because .... **(3 marks)**

2 The image shows an electron micrograph of part of a human liver cell.

(a) Explain why this is a eukaryotic cell.

....

....

....**(2 marks)**

mitochondrion

nucleus

2 μm

(b) Estimate the size of the following parts of the cell:

(i) the nucleus

.... **(2 marks)**

(ii) the mitochondrion

.... **(2 marks)**

(c) Explain why it would be possible to see the nucleus clearly using a light microscope, but the mitochondria would be unclear.

....

....

.... **(3 marks)**

3 A scientist wants to study some bacteria that are 2.5 μm long. She can use either a light microscope (the one in the lab has a magnification of ×1000) or an electron microscope (the one in the lab next door has a magnification of ×100 000).

(a) Calculate the size of the magnified image of the bacteria seen with each type of microscope.

> Remember that 1 μm = 0.000 001 m and do a reality check on your answer. The magnified image must be **bigger** than the bacteria and the image formed by the electron microscope must be **bigger** than that formed by the light microscope.

(3 marks)

(b) Explain which microscope would be better for her to use.

....

....

.... **(2 marks)**

> State which is better **and** give a reason.

Dealing with numbers

1 Give the following units in order of increasing size:

metre   micrometre   millimetre   nanometre   picometre

Guided

picometre .... metre   **(1 mark)**

2 Complete the table to convert the quantities to the units shown.

Guided

Quantity	Converted quantity	
0.005 nanometres	5	picometres
250 milligrams		grams
250 milligrams		kilograms
2.5 metres		millimetres

(4 marks)

3 For each of the following conversions, state whether it is true or false.

Guided

Conversion	True or false?
$0.000\,125\,mm = 0.125\,\mu m$	true
$150\,000\,mg = 0.015\,kg$	
$1\,kg = 10\,000\,000\,\mu g$	
$0.25\,mm = 2.5 \times 10^2\,\mu m$	

(4 marks)

4 Calculate for each of the following the actual size of the structure.

> $1\,mm = 1\,000\,\mu m$, and $1\,mm = 1\,000\,000\,nm$ (check back on page 4 of the Revision Guide).

(a) a ribosome that measured 30.9 mm in an electron micrograph
     (magnification = ×1 000 000)

.... nm   **(2 marks)**

(b) a mitochondrion that measured 163 mm in an electron micrograph
     (magnification = ×250 000)

.... nm   **(2 marks)**

(c) a nucleus that measured 7.8 mm in a light microscope (magnification = ×800)

.... μm   **(2 marks)**

Practical skills **Using a light microscope**

1 (a) State the function of the following parts of a light microscope:

(i)   the mirror

.... **(1 mark)**

(ii) the stage with clips

.... **(1 mark)**

(iii) the coarse focusing wheel

.... **(1 mark)**

(b) Give the reasons for the following precautions when using a light microscope.

(i)   Never use the coarse focusing wheel with a high power objective.

....

.... **(1 mark)**

(ii) Never point the mirror directly at the Sun.

....

.... **(1 mark)**

(c) (i)   State an alternative light source that might be safer than the Sun.

.... **(1 mark)**

> **Guided**

(ii) State **two** other precautions that you should take when using a light microscope.

precaution 1   Always start with the lowest power objective under the eyepiece.

precaution 2   ....

.... **(2 marks)**

2 You are observing a slide under high power but cannot see the part you need. Describe how you would bring the required part into view.

> Think about why you cannot see what you need and then the steps you must follow to find it. Remember some of the precautions you have to take.

....

....

....

....

.... **(3 marks)**

Drawing labelled diagrams

1 A student was given the slide below left and told to make a high power drawing to show cells in different stages of mitosis. His drawing is shown below right.

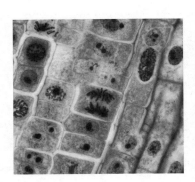

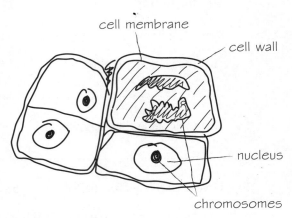

> **Guided**

(a) Identify three faults with the student's drawing.

fault 1   The drawing is in pen rather than in ....

fault 2   ....

fault 3   .... **(3 marks)**

(b) Draw your own labelled diagram of the slide above.

> Include outlines of all cells with more detail of cells showing different stages of mitosis. Try to show one of each stage.

(4 marks)

2 The student used a scale to measure the actual width of the field of view shown in the slide (above left) and found it was 0.113 mm. Calculate the magnification.

magnification = ... **(3 marks)**

Enzymes

29/4/22

1   The enzyme invertase digests sucrose to glucose and fructose. Explain why invertase will not digest the sugar lactose.

> Guided

The shape of ...the enzyme must match the shape of...

~~matches the shape of~~ ...the active site for digestion to work....

....

so ......invertase...... cannot combine with ...sugar lactose.....

....

(2 marks)

2   The graph shows how the activity of an enzyme changes with temperature. The enzyme activity is greatest at the temperature labelled B.

(a) Give the optimum temperature for this enzyme.

40°C

.... **(1 mark)**

(b) Why does the enzyme activity decrease in the region labelled C?

☐ **A**   Enzymes are killed at high temperatures.

☐ **B**   The active site cannot change shape.

☐ **C**   The substrate molecules move more slowly.

☒ **D**   The active site breaks up and the enzyme is denatured.
(1 mark)

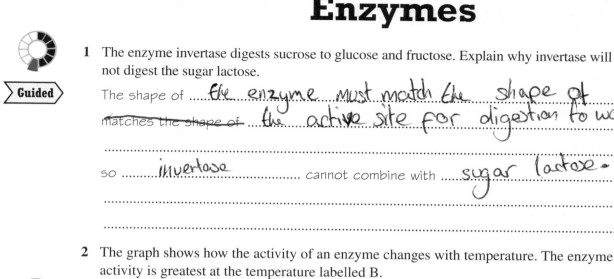

> Think about the rate of collisions involving molecules as the temperature increases.

(c) Explain why the enzyme activity increases in the region labelled A.

Activity increases at point A because the substrate ~~molecu~~ molecules move more quickly as the °C increases. **(2 marks)**

3   Amylase is an enzyme that digests starch. Its optimum pH is about 7. Pepsin and trypsin are enzymes that digest proteins. Pepsin is produced in the stomach (pH 2). Trypsin is found in pancreatic juice (pH 8.6), which is released into the small intestine. The graph shows the effect of pH on the activity of these enzymes.

Use this information to explain why proteins are digested in the stomach and small intestine.

Proteins are digested in the stomach and small intestine to prevent the pepsin and trypsin from denaturing.

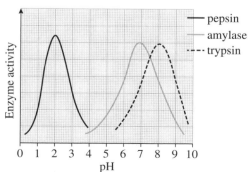

(3 marks)

7

Practical skills **pH and enzyme activity**

1 A student carried out an experiment to investigate the effect of pH on the activity of the enzyme trypsin using pieces of photographic film. Trypsin digests the protein in the film and causes the film to turn clear. Measuring the time it takes for the film to clear allows you to calculate the rate of reaction. The student used the apparatus shown.

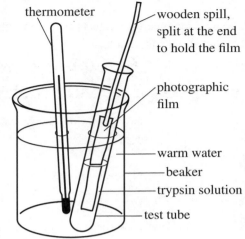

This procedure was repeated using trypsin solution at different pH values. The student's results are shown in the table.

Guided

pH	2	4	6	8	10
Time (min)	> 10	7.5	3.6	1.2	8.3
Rate/min	0	0.13			

Remember, rate = 1/time

(a) Complete the table by calculating the rate of reaction at each pH. **(2 marks)**

(b) Complete the graph to show the effect of pH on the rate of reaction.

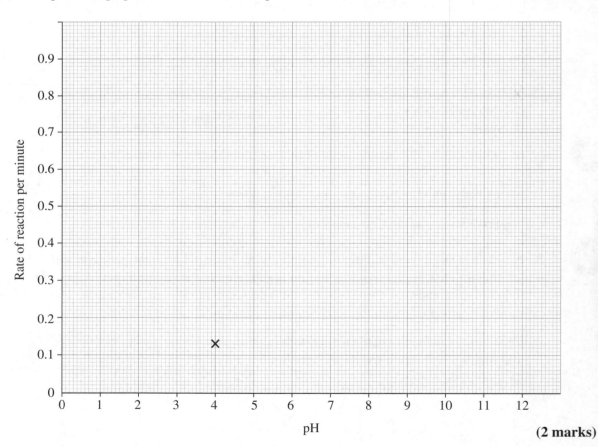

(2 marks)

(c) State **two** ways in which the experiment could be improved.

improvement 1 ....

improvement 2 .... **(2 marks)**

The importance of enzymes

1 Complete the following table.

Enzyme	Digests	Product(s)
amylase	starch	
lipase		
protease		amino acids

(3 marks)

2 (a) Explain why different digestive enzymes are needed in the digestive system.

....

....

.... **(2 marks)**

(b) Explain the importance of enzymes as biological catalysts in building the molecules needed in cells and tissues.

....

....

.... **(2 marks)**

3 Biological washing powders contain enzymes that help to break down food stains on clothes.

(a) Eggs are rich in protein. An egg fried in oil is spilled on a shirt, causing a stain. Complete the table to show the enzyme or enzymes needed to remove this stain. Place a tick (✓) in each correct box.

Enzyme	Needed to remove the stain? (✓)
amylase	
lipase	
protease	

(1 mark)

(b) Explain why biological washing powders work better below 40 °C.

....   ┌─────────────────────────────────┐
                                                              │ Think about what biological washing powders │
....   │ contain and what effect temperature might have. │
                                                              └─────────────────────────────────┘

....

.... **(3 marks)**

4 Give **one** similarity and **one** difference between digestion and synthesis in living organisms.

....

....

....

.... **(3 marks)**

🧪 Practical skills **Using reagents in food tests**

1 (a) (i) State **one** safety precaution when carrying out food tests.

.... **(1 mark)**

(ii) State **one** hazard associated with the test for starch.

.... **(1 mark)**

Guided (b) Describe how you would test for the presence of lipids (fats and oils) in a sample of food.

Mix the food with ethanol ....

....

....

....

.... **(3 marks)**

2 A student carried out a test on a concentrated solution of a reducing sugar. He added a small volume of Benedict's solution, then heated the mixture in a test tube for about five minutes.

(a) What colour change would be seen in this food test?

☐ **A** blue to green

☐ **B** blue to orange

☐ **C** blue to red

☐ **D** red to blue **(1 mark)**

(b) Describe how the student can safely heat the mixture.

> A Bunsen burner is not necessary to carry out these tests.

....

.... **(2 marks)**

3 A student analysed a broad bean. She ground up the bean, then tested the powder for food substances.

(a) The student mixed some bean powder with water, then added potassium hydroxide solution and copper sulfate solution. The mixture was pale purple. Give the meaning of this result.

.... **(1 mark)**

(b) Describe the test the student would use to find out if the broad bean contained starch.

> Say what she would do and what she would see.

....

.... **(2 marks)**

Using calorimetry

1   A student carried out an experiment to measure the energy in a potato snack. He added 20 cm³ of water to a boiling tube and measured its temperature. He used a mounted needle to hold a piece of burning potato snack underneath the boiling tube of water.

(a)   Give one further measurement needed to determine the increase in temperature of the water.

.... **(1 mark)**

(b)   The student repeated the experiment with a different snack food. Give **two** variables, other than the volume of water used, that the student should control.

> Think about the variables that the student should keep the same to ensure that any difference should only be due to the food used.

1 ....

2 .... **(2 marks)**

(c)   The table shows the student's results.

⟩ **Guided** ⟩

	Snack A	Snack B
Mass of food burnt (g)	2.5	2.0
Temperature rise of water (°C)	35	27
Energy value of food sample (J)	2940	
Energy value of food (J/g)	1200	

> Always show your working. You may get credit for a correct method even if you get a wrong answer.

(i)   Calculate the energy value of each food sample in J. Write your answers into the table.

Use this equation:

energy (J) = mass of water (g) × 4.2 × temperature rise (°C)

Snack A: energy = 20 × 4.2 × 35 = 2940 J

Snack B: energy = ... × 4.2 × .... = ... J   **(2 marks)**

(ii)   Use your answers to part (i) to calculate the energy value of each food sample in J/g. Give your answers to 2 significant figures, and write them into the table.

Snack A: energy = 2940/2.5 = 1176 J/g

= 1200 J/g to 2 significant figures

Snack B:

....

.... **(4 marks)**

(d)   The label on the packet for Snack A says that it contains 2900 J/g. Give one reason, other than a mistake, that explains why the student's results gives a lower value.

....

.... **(1 mark)**

Getting in and out of cells

1 Define diffusion.

....

....

....

.... **(2 marks)**

2 The table shows some features of two transport processes. Complete the table by placing a tick (✓) in each correct box to show the features of diffusion and of active transport.

> **Guided**

Feature	Diffusion	Active transport
Involves the movement of particles	✓	✓
Requires energy		
Can happen across a partially permeable membrane		
Net movement down a concentration gradient		

(4 marks)

3 (a) Explain what is meant by the term **osmosis**.

> **Guided**

> Make sure you use the terms 'water', 'partially permeable membrane' and 'movement' in your answer.

Osmosis is the net movement of .... across a

....

from a low ....

to a high .... **(4 marks)**

(b) The blood in the lung capillaries has a lower concentration of oxygen than the air. Oxygen moves from the air to the blood. Name the transport process involved, and give a reason that explains your answer.

....

....

....

....

....

.... **(2 marks)**

(c) Starch in food is digested to glucose. It is important that all the glucose produced is absorbed from the small intestine. Explain why this process requires energy.

....

....

....

.... **(2 marks)**

Practical skills Osmosis in potatoes

> Guided

1 Describe how you would investigate osmosis in potatoes using potato pieces. You are provided with solutions of different sucrose concentrations. You should include at least **two** steps that you should use to ensure the accuracy of your results.

Cut pieces of potato, making sure ....

....

....

Remove from the solution, then ....

.... **(4 marks)**

2 The table shows the results of an experiment to investigate osmosis in potatoes using different concentrations of sucrose.

Concentration (mol dm^{-3})	Initial mass (g)	Final mass (g)	Change in mass (g)	Percentage change in mass (%)
0	2.60	2.85		9.6
0.2	2.51	2.67	0.16	6.4
0.4	2.65	2.72	0.07	2.6
0.6	2.52	2.45	−0.07	−2.8
0.8	2.58	2.43	−0.15	

> Guided

Maths skills

(a) Calculate the two missing values in the table. Use these values to complete the table.

2.85 − 2.60 = ... g

Percentage change in mass = (−0.15/2.58) × 100 = ... %

(2 marks)

Maths skills

(b) Complete the graph to show the percentage change in mass against sucrose concentration.

(2 marks)

Draw a line of best fit. This can be curved or straight, depending on the data, but should ignore points that are clearly anomalies.

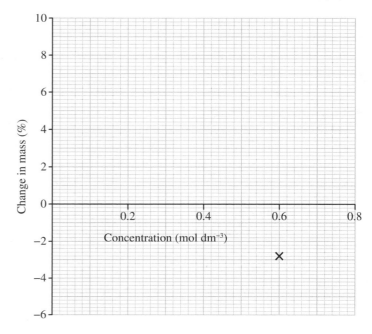

(c) Use the completed graph to estimate the concentration of the potato tissue.

.... **(1 mark)**

Extended response – Key concepts

The diagrams show a bacterial cell and a plant cell. The diagrams are not drawn to scale.

Bacterial cell

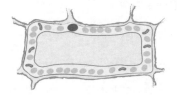

Plant cell

Compare the structures of these two cells, including subcellular structures and their functions.

> In your answer to this question, you need to think about:
>
> • the similarities between the cells
>
> • the differences between the cells.
>
> For each structure that you identify, remember to describe its function.
>
> It may help if you make a brief plan before you start writing.

....

....

....

....

....

....

....

....

....

....

....

....

....

....

....

....

.... **(6 marks)**

Mitosis

1 (a) Read the following statements about mitosis. Which statement is correct?
Tick **one** box.

  ☐ **A** A parent cell divides to produce two genetically different diploid daughter cells.

  ☐ **B** A parent cell divides to produce two genetically identical diploid daughter cells.

  ☐ **C** A parent cell divides to produce four genetically identical haploid daughter cells.

  ☐ **D** A parent cell divides to produce four genetically different haploid cells.   **(1 mark)**

(b) List the stages of mitosis in the order they happen, starting with interphase.

.... **(1 mark)**

2 Give **three** reasons why mitosis takes place.

> **Guided**

1 To produce new individuals by .... reproduction.

2 ....

3 .... **(3 marks)**

3 The photograph shows a slide of cells from an onion root tip at different stages in mitosis.

(a) Name the two stages of mitosis labelled A and B.

A ....

B .... **(2 marks)**

(b) Give a reason for each answer in part (a).

A ....

B .... **(2 marks)**

Cell growth and differentiation

1 (a) Give the name of a fertilised egg in animals.

.... **(1 mark)**

(b) State the type of cell division that occurs after an egg is fertilised.

.... **(1 mark)**

2 Plant cells divide by mitosis.

(a) State the name of the type of plant tissue where mitosis occurs rapidly.

> Remember that plants grow when cells divide and when cells elongate.

.... **(1 mark)**

(b) Describe how plant cells increase in size following mitosis.

....

.... **(2 marks)**

3 (a) Complete the table to show whether the different specialised cells are animal or plant cells.

Guided

Type of specialised cell	Animal or plant
sperm	animal
xylem	
ciliated cell	
root hair cell	
egg cell	

(3 marks)

(b) Give the name of one other type of specialised cell found in **plants** and one in **animals**.

plants ....

animals .... **(2 marks)**

4 Growth in animals happens over a particular period of the animal's lifespan. Growth happens through cell division and when cells in the animal differentiate.

(a) Explain what is meant by the term **differentiate**.

Guided   Cells become .... to perform ....

.... **(2 marks)**

(b) Give **one** reason that explains why cell differentiation is important in animals.

....

....

.... **(2 marks)**

Growth and percentile charts

1   A midwife will measure the growth of a baby in different ways. The graph shows some percentile charts for the head circumference measurement for young children.

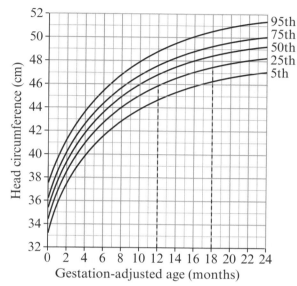

> Graphs like this sometimes look complicated – but remember that the curves are all labelled, so you can see what each one refers to.

> Note that dashed guidelines have been put in to help you answer part (b). These help to show how you get the reading for both measurements from the graph – you can then subtract one number from the other to get the final answer.

(a)   The median head circumference is described by the line where half the babies have a greater circumference, and half have the same or a smaller circumference. Which percentile curve shows the median rate of growth for babies?

☐ **A** 5th percentile   ☐ **B** 25th percentile   ☐ **C** 50th percentile   ☐ **D** 75th percentile

(1 mark)

(b)   Use the graph to calculate the change in head circumference for a baby that lies on the 25th percentile curve between 12 and 18 months old. Show your working.

change in circumference .... cm   **(2 marks)**

2   Growth in seedlings can be investigated by measuring the mass of seedlings of different ages.

> Guided

(a)   One seedling increased in mass from 12.75 g to 15.35 g over a period of 7 days. Calculate the percentage increase in mass for this seedling. Show your working.

15.35 – 12.75 = ...g

(.............../12.75) × 100 = ... %   **(2 marks)**

(b)   Describe **one** other way you could measure the growth of the seedlings.

....

....

....

....   **(2 marks)**

Stem cells

1 Plants and animals have stem cells.

(a) What is a stem cell?

☐ **A** an undifferentiated cell

☐ **B** a specialised cell of an organism

> Option D cannot be correct because stem cells may be able to help conditions such as these.

☐ **C** a cell found only in embryo plants and animals

☐ **D** ~~a cell that causes Parkinson's disease and some types of blindness~~ **(1 mark)**

(b) (i) Give the name of the tissue where plant stem cells are found.

.... **(1 mark)**

(ii) Name **two** places in a plant where you would find stem cells.

.... and .... **(2 marks)**

2 (a) Describe **one** function of adult stem cells.

....

.... **(1 mark)**

(b) Describe **one** difference between an embryonic stem cell and a differentiated cell.

....

.... **(1 mark)**

> To answer the following questions, think about what happens in a tissue transplant as well as what the different types of stem cell are capable of.

3 Parkinson's disease is caused by the death of some types of nerve cells in the brain.

(a) Describe how embryonic stem cells could be used to treat Parkinson's disease.

....

.... **(2 marks)**

(b) IPSCs are stem cells produced by modifying a patient's own skin cells. IPSCs could also be used to treat Parkinson's disease in the future.

(i) Give **one** benefit of using IPSCs rather than embryonic stem cells for treating disease.

> Benefits could involve addressing ethical concerns or practical ones.

.... **(1 mark)**

(ii) Suggest **one** risk of using IPSCs.

.... **(1 mark)**

The brain and spinal cord

1 (a) Name the two parts of the central nervous system.

.... **(1 mark)**

(b) Describe **one** function of each of the following parts of the brain:

(i) medulla oblongata

.... **(1 mark)**

(ii) cerebellum

.... **(1 mark)**

(c) Describe **two** functions of the cerebral hemispheres.

....

.... **(2 marks)**

2 Complete the table to show the part or parts of the central nervous system responsible for each activity.

> Make sure that you can tell the difference between voluntary movement (movement you think about) and involuntary movement (that you do without having to think about it).

Activity	Part of the central nervous system
increasing breathing rate during exercise	
watching a video	
playing the piano	
revising for exams	

(4 marks)

3 Sarah goes for a run while listening to her MP3 player. During the run she recognises a friend across the road and waves to her.

Guided

Describe the functions of the different parts of Sarah's brain during her run.

Her running is coordinated by the .... which controls

.... and keeps her balanced.

The .... interpret the sensory information from her

ears while listening to music and also from her eyes when she sees her friend.

Her heart rate and breathing rate are controlled by the ....

Waving to her friend is controlled by the .... **(4 marks)**

4 A man was involved in an accident. His back suffered damage that cut his spinal cord.

Suggest an effect of this damage to the spinal cord. Give a reason that explains your answer.

> Your answer should concentrate on the physical effects of spinal cord damage, rather than its psychological effects. Make sure you justify your answer.

....

....

....

.... **(4 marks)**

Neurones

1 Draw **one** line from each type of neurone to its correct function.

Neurone

motor neurone

relay neurone

sensory neurone

Function

carries impulses from one part of the central nervous system to another

carries impulses to the central nervous system

carries impulses from the central nervous system to effectors

(3 marks)

2 The diagram shows a sensory neurone.

A ....

B ....

C ....

D ....

E ....

F ....

Label the parts A – F of the sensory neurone. Write your answers on the diagram.   **(3 marks)**

3 Explain how the structure of a motor neurone is related to its function.

Guided

The axon is long so it can ....

The axon has a myelin sheath which ....

The nerve ending transmits impulses to ....   **(3 marks)**

4 The table shows the speed at which nerve impulses are carried along two types of neurone.

(a) Explain why the speed of transmission is different in the two types of neurone.

Type of neurone	Speed of transmission (m/s)
myelinated	25
unmyelinated	3

....

....   **(2 marks)**

(b) In multiple sclerosis (MS), the myelin sheath surrounding neurones in the spinal cord is destroyed. Explain what effect this would have on the movement of a person with MS.

....

....   **(2 marks)**

Responding to stimuli

1   Choose **three** words from the box to complete the sentence about the features of reflex actions.

innate	slow	automatic	conscious	learned	rapid

Reflex actions are ...., ..., and .... **(3 marks)**

2   The diagram shows a junction where neurone X meets neurone Y.

electrical impulse
axon of neurone X
gap between neurone X and neurone Y
neurone Y
electrical impulses to muscle

(a)   State the name given to the junction between two neurones.

.... **(1 mark)**

(b)   Explain which neurone (X or Y) on the diagram is a motor neurone. Give a reason for your answer.

....

.... **(2 marks)**

Guided

(c)   Describe how neurones X and Y communicate.

When an electrical impulse reaches the end of neurone X it causes the release

of .... into the gap between the neurones. This substance

.... across the .... and causes neurone Y to

.... **(4 marks)**

3   The diagram shows a reflex arc.

(a)   Describe the pathway taken by the nerve impulse in this reflex arc.

sensory neurone
stimulus
central nervous system
effector organ – muscle in the eyelid

....

....

....

....

.... **(3 marks)**

(b)   What is the stimulus in this reflex arc? Give a reason for your answer.

> 'Give a reason' means that you have to say something that supports your answer.

....

.... **(2 marks)**

The eye

1

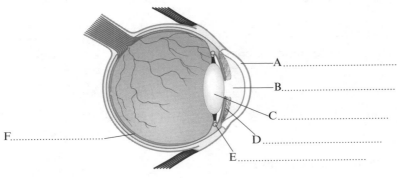

A ....
B ....
C ....
D ....
E ....
F ....

(a) Label the parts A – F on the diagram of the eye.   **(3 marks)**

(b) Explain how the structures of parts A and C are related to their function.

....

....

....

....   **(3 marks)**

Guided

2 Explain how the iris is adapted to its function.

The iris changes its size by ....

.... It does

this to control ....   **(2 marks)**

Guided

3 (a) Light from a distant object falls on the eye.

Describe what happens to the light rays when they enter the eye so that they form a sharp image.

To form an image the light rays must .... onto the ....

This occurs as ....

....   **(3 marks)**

(b) Describe what happens in the eye to allow it to focus on an object that is close.

....

....   **(2 marks)**

4 Explain why animals that hunt at night have mostly rod cells in their retinas.

> The question only mentions rod cells, but you will need to talk about cone cells as well in your answer.

....

....

....

....

....   **(3 marks)**

Eye problems

1 The diagram shows a lens in spectacles correcting a sight problem and producing a sharp image on the retina.

(a) State the sight problem being corrected in the diagram.

.... **(1 mark)**

(b) Explain why the sight correction shown in the diagram is successful.

> **Guided**

The lens makes the light rays .... so that the image moves

.... **(2 marks)**

(c) (i) State a precaution that must be taken if using contact lenses instead of spectacles to correct sight problems.

.... **(1 mark)**

(ii) Contact lenses allow oxygen to pass through them. Give a reason why this is necessary.

Remember that the cornea is made up of living cells.

.... **(1 mark)**

2 A cataract is an eye defect in which part of the lens becomes cloudy. Suggest a likely symptom of a having a cataract, and give a reason that explains your answer.

....

....

.... **(2 marks)**

3 Explain why many people need reading glasses as they get older.

> **Guided**

As they get older the lens does not ....

and so they cannot focus on .... **(2 marks)**

4 (a) State the type of cell in the retina that detects colour.

.... **(1 mark)**

(b) Describe the cause of red–green colour blindness.

....

.... **(2 marks)**

Extended response – Cells and control

Fertilisation of a human egg cell produces a zygote, a single cell that eventually gives rise to every different type of cell in an adult human.

Describe the role of mitosis in the growth and development of a zygote into an adult human.

> You will be more successful in extended response questions if you plan your answer before you start writing. Take care, because the question mentions fertilisation but it is really about growth and specialisation. Do not be tempted to talk about sexual reproduction – that is in the next topic.
>
> Your answer should include the following:
>
> • mitosis and cell division causing growth (from embryo to adult), and its importance in repair and replacement of cells
>
> • cell differentiation to produce specialised cells
>
> • the role of stem cells in the embryo as well as in the adult.
>
> Do not forget to use appropriate scientific terminology. Here are some of the words you should include in your answer:
>
>   cell cycle   replication   diploid   daughter cells   specialise   differentiate

....

....

....

....

....

....

....

....

....

....

....

....

....

....

.... **(6 marks)**

Asexual and sexual reproduction

1   Complete the table to compare features of sexual and asexual forms of reproduction.

Feature	Sexual reproduction	Asexual reproduction
need to find a mate		
mixing of genetic information	mixes genetic information from each parent	no mixing of genetic information
characteristics of offspring		

(3 marks)

2   During the growing season, strawberry plants send out runners. Where a runner touches the ground a new plant develops. Later in the summer the original plant produces flowers that are fertilised and produce fruits with seeds. Animals eat the fruits and deposit them in their faeces far from the original plant.

(a) Explain which of these is sexual reproduction and which is asexual reproduction.

> 'Explain' means that you must identify each type of reproduction **and** give a reason.

runners ....

....

fruits ....

.... **(4 marks)**

(b) Give **one** benefit to the strawberry plant of each type of reproduction.

> Make sure that you give a benefit and say why it is a benefit for each type of reproduction.

....

....

.... **(2 marks)**

(c) Give **one** disadvantage to the strawberry plant of each type of reproduction.

....

....

.... **(2 marks)**

3   Describe **two** ways in which sexual reproduction requires organisms to expend more energy compared to asexual reproduction.

....

....

.... **(2 marks)**

Meiosis

1 Human gametes are haploid cells. During sexual reproduction, the gametes fuse to produce a zygote.

(a) Describe what is meant by:

(i) haploid

.... **(1 mark)**

(ii) gametes

.... **(1 mark)**

(b) State the name of the male sex cells and the female sex cells in humans.

male ....

female .... **(2 marks)**

2 A cell contains 20 chromosomes. It divides by meiosis.

(a) State the number of chromosomes in each daughter cell.

.... **(1 mark)**

(b) Explain why the daughter cells are not genetically identical.

....

.... **(2 marks)**

3 The diagram below shows a cell with two pairs of chromosomes undergoing meiosis.

parent
cell

(a) State the name of the process indicated by letter **A** in the diagram.

.... **(1 mark)**

(b) Complete the diagram above to show how daughter cells are formed. **(3 marks)**

> Use the drawing as a guide. Make sure that you draw the chromosomes as they are shown, paying attention to the relative sizes.

4 Describe the importance of the two types of cell division, mitosis and meiosis.

Guided

Mitosis maintains the ...., and produces cells that are

.... to the parent cell. It is used for ....

Meiosis creates .... that have .... the

number of .... Fertilisation restores the

.... **(5 marks)**

DNA

1 Our chromosomes contain genetic information. This information is held in our DNA.

(a) State the name used to describe all the DNA of an organism.

.... **(1 mark)**

(b) Describe the difference between chromosomes, genes and DNA.

> This question is best answered by thinking of the definition of each of these terms.

Guided

A chromosome consists of a long molecule of ....

....

.... **(3 marks)**

2 (a) What name is given to the shape of a DNA molecule?

.... **(1 mark)**

(b) The DNA molecule is made up of a series of bases.

(i) State the number of different bases present in DNA.

.... **(1 mark)**

(ii) Describe how the two strands of the DNA molecule are linked together.

....

.... **(1 mark)**

3 The diagram shows a section of DNA.

(a) DNA is a polymer. Give **one** piece of evidence from the diagram that DNA is a polymer.

....

....

(1 mark)

A ....

B ....

C ....

(b) Identify the components A, B and C of the DNA structure. Write your answers on the diagram.   **(3 marks)**

> You will not be expected to draw this structure from memory, but you may be expected to label the parts shown.

4 The sequence of bases on one strand of DNA is ATGGTC. What is the order of the complementary bases on the other strand?

☐ **A** TACCAG

☐ **B** CATTAG

☐ **C** GCAACT

☐ **D** CTGGTA   **(1 mark)**

Gregor Mendel

1   Before the work of Mendel, scientists thought that 'blending' caused variation in inherited characteristics.

   (a)   Describe how characteristics such as red hair could not be explained by 'blending' of the parents' characteristics.

    ....

    ....   **(2 marks)**

   (b)   In his work with pea plants, Mendel chose to work with characteristics such as pea shape (round or wrinkled), pea colour (yellow or green) or plant height (tall or short). Explain the importance of his choice of characteristics.

> **Guided**

    These could not be caused by .... because ....

    ....   **(2 marks)**

2   Mendel carried out experiments with pea plants. In Experiment 1, he started with pure-bred plants that produced yellow seeds. He crossed these plants with pure-bred plants that produced green seeds.
In Experiment 2, he crossed pure-bred plants that produced round seeds with pure-bred plants that produced wrinkled seeds. In both experiments, he crossed plants from the first generation with each other to produce a second generation. The table shows his results.

	Experiment 1		Experiment 2	
Parents	yellow seeds	green seeds	round seeds	wrinkled seeds
First generation	all yellow seeds		all round seeds	
Second generation	349 yellow seeds	112 green seeds	595 round seeds	193 wrinkled seeds

> In each of the following questions you need to **explain**, so make sure that you give some evidence to support your answer.

   (a)   Explain why it was important that Mendel used pure-bred seeds.

    ....

    ....   **(2 marks)**

   (b)   Give a suitable conclusion from the results of each experiment, and give a reason for each conclusion.

    Experiment 1 ....

    ....

    Experiment 2 ....

    ....   **(4 marks)**

   (c)   In a third experiment, Mendel took pure-bred plants with yellow round seeds and crossed them with pure-bred plants with green wrinkled seeds. Predict what type of seeds would have been produced in the first generation.

    ....   **(1 mark)**

Genetic terms

1 Eye colour in humans can be controlled by two alleles of the eye colour gene. One recessive allele (b) codes for blue and one dominant allele (B) codes for brown.

> You need to know what recessive, genotype, phenotype, homozygous and heterozygous mean.

(a) (i)   State what is meant by alleles.

.... **(1 mark)**

(ii) Using eye colour as an example, explain the difference between the terms **genotype** and **phenotype**.

....

....

....

.... **(2 marks)**

(b) State the following genotypes for eye colour:

homozygous blue: ....

homozygous brown: ....

heterozygous: .... **(3 marks)**

(c) A girl has blue eyes. Explain what her genotype must be.

....

.... **(2 marks)**

2 Mendel used the results from his experiments to devise his three laws of inheritance.
1. Each gamete receives only one factor for a characteristic.
2. The version of a factor that a gamete receives is random and does not depend on the other factors in the gamete.
3. Some versions of a factor are more powerful than others and always have an effect in the offspring.
Mendel did not know what these 'factors' actually were.
Explain how our understanding of genes and chromosomes has confirmed his laws.

Guided There are two copies of each chromosome in body cells ....

....

....

....

....

.... **(4 marks)**

Monohybrid inheritance

1   Two plants both have the genotype Tt. The two plants are bred together.

The allele that makes the plants grow tall is represented by T, and the allele that makes plants shorter is represented by t.

> Percentage probabilities from Punnett squares will always be 0, 25%, 50%, 75% or 100%, depending on the number of squares with a particular genotype (0, 1, 2, 3 or 4 squares). In fractions, probabilities will always be 0, $\frac{1}{4}$, $\frac{1}{2}$, $\frac{3}{4}$ or 1.

(a)   Complete the Punnett square to give the gametes of the parents and the genotypes of the offspring.

gametes of parent 1

gametes of parent 2

> Take great care to complete the square correctly and use the right letters.

(2 marks)

(b)   State and explain the percentage of the offspring from this cross that will be short.

> **Guided**

25% of the offspring from this cross will be short. I know this because

....

.... **(3 marks)**

(c)   Determine the probability of the offspring from this cross being tall. Express your answer as a fraction.

....

.... **(1 mark)**

2   Fur colour in mice is controlled by two alleles, G and g. Two mice with different fur colour produced a total of 40 offspring.

(a)   Complete the Punnett square for this cross.

		Parent genotype Gg	
	Parent gametes		
Parent genotype gg			

(2 marks)

(b)   Homozygous recessive mice have white fur. Predict the expected number of offspring with white fur.

> Recessive alleles are shown with lowercase letters.

.... **(1 mark)**

Family pedigrees

1 Two healthy parents have a child who has sickle-cell anaemia, a condition caused by a recessive allele. Which **one** of the following is true?

> Questions like this can be tricky! Some answers might be true in general, but not in this particular case. You need to pick the one that is true **and** applies to this example.

☐ **A** Both parents are homozygous for the sickle-cell allele.

☐ **B** One parent is homozygous for the sickle-cell allele and the other is homozygous for the normal allele.

☐ **C** Both parents are heterozygous for the sickle-cell allele.

☐ **D** One parent is heterozygous for the sickle-cell allele and the other is homozygous for the normal allele.

(1 mark)

2 This family pedigree shows the inheritance of cystic fibrosis (CF).

CF is a genetic condition in humans caused by a recessive allele.

(a) State how many cystic fibrosis alleles an individual must inherit in order to show the symptoms of CF.

....

(1 mark)

(b) State how many males in the family pedigree have a homozygous recessive genotype.

....

(1 mark)

☐ healthy male
○ healthy female
■ male with CF
● female with CF

Guided

(c) State and explain the genotype of person 4. Use F for the normal allele and f for the recessive allele.

Person 4 does not have cystic fibrosis. This means that she must have one

.... *allele from her father. But she must*

have inherited a .... *allele from her mother.*

This means that her genotype is .... **(3 marks)**

(d) Explain the evidence that cystic fibrosis is caused by a recessive allele.

> Remember that some people are carriers of an allele that causes a genetic condition. Parents who are carriers do not have the condition, but they can pass it on to their children.

....

....

.... **(2 marks)**

Sex determination

1 (a) A baby girl is born. Explain which sex chromosome was in the sperm that fertilised the egg.

....

.... **(2 marks)**

(b) (i) Complete the Punnett square to show the sex chromosomes of both parents and all possible children.

> This is a Punnett square but you could also use a genetic diagram to show how X and Y chromosomes combine.

(2 marks)

(ii) State the sex of the child in the shaded box.

.... **(1 mark)**

2 (a) A couple who have a girl wish to have a second child. Explain the chance of the couple's second child being a boy.

....

....

....

....

....

.... **(3 marks)**

(b) Read this statement:

> If a couple have had children and they are all girls, then the next child is more likely to be a boy.

Discuss whether you think this statement is correct.

....

....

....

.... **(2 marks)**

Inherited characteristics

1 Describe what is meant by codominance.

.... **(1 mark)**

2 A couple had four children, half of whom had group A blood and half of whom had group AB blood. The man was group A.

(a) State the genotype of the children.

group A blood: ....

group AB blood: .... **(2 marks)**

(b) State and explain the genotype and blood group of the mother.

> A Punnett square might help to solve this one, but is not essential.

....

....

.... **(3 marks)**

(c) The mother had a fifth child who had group B blood. Explain why the father of her first four children could not be the father of this child.

A child who is group B must receive .... *from each parent,*

.... **(2 marks)**

3 A couple both have the genotype $I^A I^B$.

(a) Complete the Punnett square below. Identify the blood group of each possible child.

		Parent genotype $I^A I^B$	
	Parent gametes	I^A	I^B
Parent genotype $I^A I^B$	I^A		
	I^B		

(3 marks)

(b) Determine the probability of each blood group.

> Don't forget that you can express probability as a percentage or a fraction.

....

....

.... **(1 mark)**

Variation and mutation

Guided

1   What are the causes of differences between the following?

(a) the masses of students in a year 7 class

Students in a year 7 class will show differences in mass caused by ....

variation as well as .... variation.   **(2 marks)**

(b) a pair of identical twins

Identical twins will show differences caused only by .... variation.   **(1 mark)**

2   Mr and Mrs Davies have six children. The table shows the heights of each of the six children when they reached adulthood.

Child	George	Arthur	Stanley	James	Josh	Peter
Adult height (cm)	181	184	178	190	193	179

(a) Calculate the mean height of the six Davies children. Show your working out. Give your answer to 1 decimal place.

mean height = ... cm   **(2 marks)**

(b) Mr Davies is 192 cm tall and Mrs Davies is 165 cm tall. Mr Davies wonders why his children show a range of different heights. Mrs Davies wonders why the mean height of the children is not the same as the mean of her height and her husband's height. Suggest an explanation that will answer their questions.

> Don't forget to cover both genetic factors and at least one environmental factor. Make sure that you use scientific language such as alleles and inheritance in your answer.

....

....

....

....

....   **(4 marks)**

3   (a) Describe what is meant by a mutation.

....

....

....   **(2 marks)**

(b) State the possible effects of a mutation on the phenotype of an organism.

....

....

....   **(2 marks)**

The Human Genome Project

1 (a) State what is meant by the human genome.

....

.... **(1 mark)**

(b) State **two** advantages and **two** disadvantages of decoding the human genome.

Guided

advantage 1

A person at risk from a genetic condition will be ....

advantage 2

....

disadvantage 1

....

disadvantage 2

.... **(4 marks)**

2 Scientists have discovered that a mutation in the human *BRCA1* gene increases a woman's risk of developing breast cancer. Give **two** benefits and **two** drawbacks to a woman of knowing that she has this mutation.

> You need to apply your knowledge and understanding to answer this question. In this case, think about how it may help a woman to know that she has the harmful mutation in the *BRCA1* gene, and why this knowledge may cause her problems or concerns.

....

....

....

....

....

....

....

.... **(4 marks)**

Extended response – Genetics

Gregor Mendel carried out his work before anything was known about DNA, genes or chromosomes. He summarised his work in three laws of inheritance:

1. Each gamete receives only one factor for a characteristic.

2. The version of a factor that a gamete receives is random and does not depend on the other factors in the gamete.

3. Some versions of a factor are more powerful than others and always have an effect in the offspring.

Describe how modern knowledge of genetics has confirmed that Mendel was correct in his conclusions.

> You will be more successful in extended writing questions if you plan your answer before you start writing.
>
> Modern genetics uses terms such as genes, chromosomes, alleles, dominant and recessive, homozygous and heterozygous. Think about how Mendel's ideas and terms can be matched to these modern ones.

....

....

....

....

....

....

....

....

....

....

....

....

....

....

....

....

....

.... **(6 marks)**

Evolution

1 (a) Describe the work of Darwin and Wallace in the development of the theory of evolution.

....

....

.... **(2 marks)**

(b) The ideas of Darwin and Wallace have important impacts on modern biology. Complete the table by placing a tick (✓) in each box that shows a correct impact of their ideas.

> **Guided**

Possible impact	Correct (✓)
Helps us understand the relationships between different species	✓
Explains how new species evolve	
Explains how life on Earth first began	
Explains how different species adapt to changes in their environment	

(2 marks)

2 Explain why, when an environment changes, some organisms within a species survive whereas others die.

> You should use scientific terms such as variation and survival in your answer.

....

....

.... **(2 marks)**

3 When a new species is discovered, a scientist may take some of its DNA to analyse. Explain how this would help establish if this is a new species.

> **Guided**

It will help .... the new species and to find out

which other ....

.... **(2 marks)**

4 It is important to complete a course of antibiotics.

Explain how stopping a course of antibiotics early can cause antibiotic resistance in bacteria.

> Darwin's theory was about natural selection and the survival of the fittest, so you should relate these to antibiotic resistance in bacteria.

....

....

....

....

.... **(4 marks)**

Human evolution

1   Apart from the differences in body hair, using the diagrams of Ardi and Lucy state three differences between them.

1. ....

2. ....

3. ....

(3 marks)

Ardi   Lucy

2   Some evidence for human evolution has come from the fossil record of the skull. The table below shows some of this evidence.

> You do not need to remember details such as brain sizes but you do need to remember the names and the general trends.

Name of species	Age of typical fossil (millions of years)	Brain volume (cm³)
Ardipithecus ramidus (Ardi)	4.4	350
Australopithecus afarensis (Lucy)	3.2	400
Homo habilis	2.4	550
Homo erectus	1.8	850

(a) Describe the relationship between when each species first appeared and brain volume.

....

.... **(2 marks)**

(b) The first stone tools are dated from about 2.4 million years ago. Using the table, deduce what may have enabled the use of stone tools.

Guided

An increase in ....

.... **(2 marks)**

3   The diagram shows two images of stone tools.

(a) Explain how scientists work out the ages of stone tools.

....

....

....

.... **(2 marks)**

A   B

(b) Using the diagram, explain how stone tool A was held. Give reasons for your answer.

....

....

.... **(3 marks)**

Classification

1   Describe the similarities between a human arm and a bat's wing that suggest humans and bats share a common ancestor.

....

.... **(2 marks)**

2   Give **two** reasons why animals and plants are placed in separate kingdoms.

> **Guided**

Plants ....

but animals ....

Plant cells have .... but .... **(2 marks)**

3   The table shows how some organisms are classified.

Classification group	Humans	Wolf	Panther
kingdom	Animalia	Animalia	Animalia
phylum	Chordata	Chordata	Chordata
class	Mammalia	Mammalia	Mammalia
order	Primate	Carnivora	Carnivora
family	Hominidae	Canidae	Felidae
genus	Homo	Canis	Panthera
species	Sapiens	Lupus	Pardus
binomial name	*Homo sapiens*	*Canis lupus*	*Panthera pardus*

Explain which two organisms in the table are most closely related.

....

....

.... **(2 marks)**

4   A classification system containing three domains has been suggested to replace the system containing five domains.

(a) Which domains are found in the three-domain system?

☐   **A**   Plants, Animals, Prokaryotes

☐   **B**   Prokaryotes, Eubacteria, Eukaryota

☐   **C**   Archaea, Eukaryota, Eubacteria

☐   **D**   Protists, Prokaryotes, Eukaryota.   **(1 mark)**

(b) Give the type of research that has led to the suggestion of a three-domain system.

> Remember that the technology to carry out this sort of research did not exist until relatively recently.

.... **(1 mark)**

Selective breeding

1 (a) Describe what is meant by selective breeding.

....

....

.... **(2 marks)**

(b) Explain how pig breeders could use selective breeding to produce lean pigs with less body fat.

> The principles of selective breeding are the same, even if you aren't familiar with this example.

....

....

....

.... **(3 marks)**

2 Food production can be increased by conventional plant breeding programmes.

(a) State **three** different characteristics that could be selected for in a crop suitable for use in any country.

....

....

....

.... **(3 marks)**

(b) State **two** other characteristics that might be selected for in a crop to be grown in a hot, dry part of Africa.

....

....

.... **(2 marks)**

3 Give **three** risks of selective breeding.

Guided

1. Alleles that might be useful in the future ....

2. ....

....

3. ....

.... **(3 marks)**

Genetic engineering

1 (a) Some potato plants have been genetically engineered so they can resist attack by insect pests. Their cells contain a gene from a different organism that produces a toxic protein. What has genetic engineering done to these potato plants?

> The phenotype of an organism is all its observable characteristics.

☐ **A** made no changes to their genome or phenotype

☐ **B** changed their phenotype but not their genome

☐ **C** changed their genome but not their phenotype

☐ **D** changed their genome and their phenotype   **(1 mark)**

(b) Resistance to insect attack is one example of a useful new characteristic given to GM crop plants.

(i) Give **one** other example of a useful new characteristic that can be given to GM crop plants.

> You do not need to name the species of crop plant involved.

.... **(1 mark)**

(ii) Give **one** advantage to a farmer of planting insect-resistant potato plants.

.... **(1 mark)**

(iii) Suggest **one** way in which the environment may be harmed by insect-resistant potato plants.

> Think about species, other than the insect pests, that may be present in or near the potato fields.

.... **(1 mark)**

2 Scientists have produced genetically modified mice that glow green in blue light. These 'glow mice' contain a gene naturally found in jellyfish. Describe how this genetically modified organism is produced.

⟩ **Guided** ⟩ The gene from a .... is cut out using ....

This gene is transferred to a .... embryo cell, and inserted into

a chromosome. The embryo is then allowed to develop as normal.   **(3 marks)**

3 People with Type 1 diabetes cannot produce insulin and need to inject themselves with this hormone. Until recently, insulin extracted from the pancreas of pigs was used. More recently, human insulin produced from GM bacteria has been used. Explain the advantages of using GM bacteria to produce the insulin for treating people with Type 1 diabetes.

....

....

....

.... **(4 marks)**

Tissue culture

1 Tissue culture is used to produce clones of a plant.

(a) Describe what clones are.

.... **(1 mark)**

(b) Give **two** reasons why plants may be cloned.

Guided

to make useful plant products such as anticancer drugs, and to ....

.... **(2 marks)**

(c) The table shows the main steps involved in tissue culture. They are not in the correct order. Complete the table to show the correct order, starting with 1 for the first step and ending with 4 for the last step.

Description of step	Order (1 to 4)
Allow samples to grow into tiny plants.	
Transfer the plants to trays of compost.	
Cut a sample of tissue from a plant.	
Transfer the sample to agar jelly containing nutrients and plant hormones.	

(2 marks)

2 A pharmaceutical company used cell culture to test a new drug for safety before giving it to humans.

(a) Describe how the company would produce the culture.

> You may need to review stem cells on page 18 of the Revision Guide.

....

....

.... **(2 marks)**

(b) Give **two** advantages of using cell culture to test a new drug, rather than testing the drug on laboratory animals.

1 ....

....

2 ....

.... **(2 marks)**

Insect-resistant plants

1   *Bacillus thuringiensis* is a bacterium that produces a substance that is poisonous to caterpillars and other insect pests.

(a)   Suggest reasons that explain why the poisonous substance is called the **Bt toxin**.

....

.... **(2 marks)**

(b)   The gene for the Bt toxin can be transferred into the genome of crop plants.

    (i)   Give a reason that explains why these genetically modified (GM) crop plants produce the Bt toxin.

.... **(1 mark)**

    (ii)   The table shows some features of these GM crop plants. Complete the table by placing a tick (✓) next to each feature that could be a disadvantage.

Feature	Disadvantage (✓)
Less chemical insecticide is needed.	
Seeds for GM plants are more expensive.	
Insects may become resistant to the BT toxin.	
Crop damage is reduced which increases yields.	
The Bt gene might transfer to wild plants by pollination.	

(3 marks)

    (iii)   Give **one** advantage of these GM crop plants compared to unmodified crop plants.

.... **(1 mark)**

2   Glyphosate is a chemical herbicide. It is used to kill weeds that compete with crop plants. Some crop plants have been genetically engineered to be resistant to glyphosate.

(a)   A farmer plants glyphosate-resistant GM wheat in a field. Weeds and wheat plants begin to grow. Describe what happens after the farmer sprays glyphosate on the field.

....

.... **(1 mark)**

(b)   Explain **one** advantage to the farmer of using this GM wheat.

    ┌──────────────────────────────┐
    │ Think about the things that plants │
    │ compete with each other for. │
    └──────────────────────────────┘

....

.... **(2 marks)**

(c)   Explain **one** advantage to the company that sells the glyphosate and GM wheat.

The company's profits could increase because ....

.... **(2 marks)**

Meeting population needs

1 State **two** agricultural solutions that attempt to meet the need for food of a growing human population.

1. ....

2. .... **(2 marks)**

2 Aphids (greenfly) are insect pests that attack many food crops, including potatoes. Two identical plots of potato plants were chosen and infested with aphids. In one plot ladybirds (natural predators of aphids) were also introduced. The graph shows the number of aphids on the potato plants in the two plots during the 10 days after infestation, either with or without ladybirds.

Make sure that you quote numerical data from the graph in your answer.

(a) Describe how the population of aphids in the absence of ladybirds changed during the 10-day period.

....

....

.... **(3 marks)**

(b) Describe and explain the differences seen when ladybirds are present on the potato plants.

> **Guided**

When ladybirds are present, the number of aphids ....

because ....

.... **(3 marks)**

3 Some farmers use an integrated approach to pest control. This involves both biological control and chemical control methods. Suggest **two** reasons why these farmers do this.

Biological controls have disadvantages; you should explain what these are and how chemical pesticides might make up for these.

.... **(2 marks)**

4 Give **one** advantage and **one** disadvantage of using artificial fertilisers.

Artificial fertilisers are manufactured chemical substances used by farmers and gardeners.

Advantage: ....

....

Disadvantage: ....

.... **(2 marks)**

Extended response – Genetic modification

Humans have improved food plants over thousands of years. Compared to wild varieties, modern crop plants usually produce larger amounts of better quality food.

Discuss how selective breeding, genetic engineering and tissue culture may be used to improve crop plants. In your answer, you do **not** need to describe how these processes are carried out.

> You will be more successful in extended response questions if you plan your answer before you start writing.
>
> It may help to think about:
>
> - which processes change plants and which do not
>
> - one or more examples of desirable changes, other than the two given to you
>
> - reasons why tissue culture might be used.

....

....

....

....

....

....

....

....

....

....

....

....

....

....

....

....

....

....

.... **(6 marks)**

Health and disease

1 According to the World Health Organization (WHO), good health is a state of 'complete physical, social and mental well-being'. State what is meant by the following terms.

(a) physical well-being

.... **(1 mark)**

(b) mental well-being

.... **(1 mark)**

(c) social well-being

.... **(1 mark)**

Guided

2 (a) Complete the table by putting a tick in the appropriate box to show whether the disease is communicable or non-communicable.

Disease	Communicable	Non-communicable
influenza ('flu')	✔	
lung cancer		
coronary heart disease		
tuberculosis		
Chlamydia (a type of STI)		

(3 marks)

(b) Explain why you identified some diseases as communicable and others as non-communicable.

....

.... **(2 marks)**

3 HIV is a virus that can infect humans. HIV makes it easier for other pathogens to infect the human body. Suggest an explanation for how HIV does this.

> Think about what types of cells are infected by the HIV virus.

....

.... **(2 marks)**

4 (a) Explain how viruses cause disease.

....

....

.... **(3 marks)**

(b) Describe **two** ways in which bacteria make us feel ill.

....

....

.... **(2 marks)**

Common infections

1 The table shows the percentage of 15 to 49 year olds with HIV in some African countries.

African country	Percentage of 15 to 49 year olds with HIV in some African countries			
	2006	2007	2008	2009
Namibia	15.0	14.3	13.7	13.1
South Africa	18.1	18.0	17.9	17.8
Zambia	13.8	13.7	13.6	13.5
Zimbabwe	17.2	16.1	15.1	14.3

(a) Identify the country with the largest decrease in the percentage of HIV between 2008 and 2009. Show your working.

> First work out what the decrease was for each country. For example, Zambia went from 13.6% to 13.5%. If you are not sure – use your calculator!

country with largest decrease .... **(2 marks)**

(b) The data for each African country follow the same overall trend. Use the data in the table to describe this trend.

....

.... **(2 marks)**

2 (a) What kind of pathogen causes Chalara ash dieback?

> **Guided**

☐ **A** ~~a virus~~   ☐ **C** a protist

☐ **B** a bacterium   ☐ **D** a fungus   **(1 mark)**

(b) Describe the effects of the pathogen on the trees.

....

.... **(2 marks)**

3 The table shows several diseases, the type of pathogen that causes them and the symptoms (signs of infection). Complete the table by filling in the gaps.

Disease	Type of pathogen	Signs of infection
cholera		watery faeces
	bacterium	persistent cough – may cough up blood-speckled mucus
malaria		
HIV		mild flu-like symptoms at first

(3 marks)

4 *Helicobacter* is a pathogen that causes stomach ulcers.

(a) State the type of pathogen involved.

.... **(1 mark)**

(b) Describe the symptoms it causes in infected people.

.... **(2 marks)**

How pathogens spread

1 Which of these statements about malaria is correct?

☐ **A** Malaria is caused by a mosquito that invades liver cells.

☐ **B** The malaria pathogen is a mosquito.

☐ **C** The malaria pathogen is a protist that is spread by a vector, the mosquito.

☐ **D** The malaria pathogen is a mosquito that is spread by a vector, the protist.   **(1 mark)**

2 Complete the table to show ways in which the spread of certain pathogens can be reduced.

Disease	Pathogen	Ways to reduce or prevent its spread
Ebola haemorrhagic fever		Keep infected people isolated; wear full protective clothing while working with infected people or dead bodies.
tuberculosis	bacterium	

(2 marks)

3 Cholera is a disease that can spread rapidly in disaster areas when drinking water supplies are damaged. Explain **one** way that its spread could be reduced or prevented.

....

....

....

....   **(2 marks)**

4 (a) Explain why bacterial diseases such as cholera are less common in developed countries.

> Think about how these diseases are spread and how developed countries are able to control them.

....

....

....

....   **(2 marks)**

(b) Explain why, during the 2014–15 Ebola outbreak, health workers wore full body protection when handling dead bodies.

Guided

To prevent being infected ....

because Ebola virus is present ....

....

....   **(2 marks)**

STIs

1 State what is meant by an STI.

....

.... **(1 mark)**

2 *Chlamydia* is a pathogen that causes an STI. Which of these statements is correct?

☐ **A** *Chlamydia* is a virus.

☐ **B** A person infected with *Chlamydia* may not realise they are infected.

☐ **C** *Chlamydia* has a lysogenic cycle.

☐ **D** *Chlamydia* cannot be passed from mother to baby during birth.   **(1 mark)**

3 Complete the table.

Guided

Mechanism of transmission	Precautions to reduce or prevent STI
unprotected sex with an infected partner	using .... during sexual intercourse
	supplying intravenous drug abusers with sterile needles
infection from blood products	

(3 marks)

4 The HIV virus has a lysogenic cycle.

(a) Describe what happens to the virus during the lysogenic cycle.

....

....

....

.... **(2 marks)**

(b) Explain why it can be many years between being infected with HIV and developing AIDS.

> Remember that viruses can multiply in two different ways.

....

....

....

.... **(2 marks)**

Human defences

1 (a) Describe the role of the skin in protecting the body from infection.

....

.... **(1 mark)**

(b) Describe **one** chemical defence against infection from what we eat or drink.

.... **(1 mark)**

(c) (i) Name an enzyme, found in tears, that protects against infection.

.... **(1 mark)**

(ii) Describe how the enzyme named in part (i) protects the eyes against infection.

....

.... **(2 marks)**

2 The diagram shows a section of epithelium in a human bronchiole, one of the tubes in the lung.

(a) (i) State the name of the substance labelled A.

.... **(1 mark)**

(ii) Describe the role of substance A in protecting the lungs from infection.

.... **(1 mark)**

(b) (i) State the name of the structure labelled B.

.... **(1 mark)**

(ii) Describe the part played by the type of cell labelled C in protecting the lungs from infection.

> **Guided**

The .... on the surface of these cells move in a wave-like motion

....

....

.... **(3 marks)**

(c) Chemicals in cigarette smoke can paralyse the structures labelled B.

Explain why this increases the risk of smokers suffering from lung infections compared with non-smokers.

....

....

.... **(2 marks)**

The immune system

1 Name the type of blood cell that produces antibodies.

Lymphocytes .... **(1 mark)**

2 Describe how lymphocytes help protect the body by attacking pathogens.

Pathogens have substances called _antigens_ on their surface. White blood

cells called _lymphocytes_ are activated if they have _antigens_ that fit

these substances. These cells then _divide_

so that They produce large amounts of antibodies that

can destroy the pathogen **(5 marks)**

3 The graph shows the concentration of antibodies in the blood of a young girl. The lines labelled A show the concentration of antibodies effective against the measles virus. The line labelled B shows the concentration of antibodies effective against the chickenpox virus.

> There is a lot to think about in this question so take it one step at a time.

(a) At the time shown by arrow 1, there was an outbreak of measles. The girl was exposed to the measles virus for the first time in her life. Explain the shape of line A in the five weeks after arrow 1.

Over the first two weeks antigens are produced until between week 2 and 3 the pathogen is destroyed. I week 3 and 4 the number of specialised lymphocytes decreases **(4 marks)**

(b) Five months later (shown by arrow 2) there was an outbreak of measles and chickenpox. The girl was exposed to both viruses. Explain the shape of line A in the five weeks after arrow 2.

....

....

.... **(3 marks)**

(c) Use lines A and B to help you answer these questions.

(i) State whether the girl had been exposed to the chickenpox virus in the past. Explain your answer.

....

.... **(2 marks)**

(ii) In the second outbreak of measles, the girl showed no symptom of measles. Explain why.

....

.... **(2 marks)**

Immunisation

Guided

1   (a)   Children are given vaccinations against many childhood infections. State what is meant by a vaccine.

A vaccine contains antigens from ....

.... **(2 marks)**

(b)   A vaccine prevents a person from becoming ill from infection with a pathogen. This works even if they are exposed to the pathogen a long time after the vaccination. Explain why.

....

....

....

.... **(3 marks)**

(c)   Describe **two** disadvantages of vaccination.

....

.... **(2 marks)**

2   In 1998 a group of doctors suggested there was a connection between the MMR (measles, mumps and rubella) vaccine and autism. This made some parents afraid of having their babies vaccinated. The graph shows how the percentage of babies in the UK who were given the MMR vaccine changed over the following years.

(a)   State which year had the lowest rate of vaccination.

....

(1 mark)

(b)   Predict what would happen to the number of children suffering from measles in the period 1998–2004. Justify your answer.

....

....

.... **(2 marks)**

(c)   The target immunisation rate for measles is 95%. Explain why it is not necessary for 100% of children to be immunised.

> This question is asking you to talk about herd immunity.

....

....

.... **(2 marks)**

Treating infections

1 (a) Which of the following statements is correct?

☐ **A** An antibiotic is produced in the body to fight infection.

☐ **B** Some antibiotics are becoming resistant to bacteria.

☐ **C** Antibiotics are medicines that kill or slow down growth of bacteria in the body.

☐ **D** Antibodies are medicines that kill or slow down growth of bacteria in the body. **(1 mark)**

(b) Explain why antibiotics can be used to treat bacterial infections in people.

....

....

.... **(2 marks)**

2 Colds are caused by viruses. A man has a very bad cold. He asks a pharmacist if an antibiotic such as penicillin would help to cure his cold.

State, with a reason, whether the pharmacist would advise the man to take penicillin.

The pharmacist's advice would be ....

The man's cold is due to a virus, so the penicillin ....

.... **(2 marks)**

3 Sinusitis causes a stuffy nose. Some patients with sinusitis were divided into two groups. One group was treated for 14 days with antibiotics whilst the other group did not receive antibiotics. Each day they were asked if they still had symptoms. The results are shown in the graph.

(a) State what you can deduce about the cause of sinusitis from the data.

> You are asked only for a deduction, not an explanation – although you might need to think about the answer to part (b) before you make your deduction!

.... **(1 mark)**

(b) Discuss whether the data supports the use of antibiotics to treat sinusitis.

> Be sure to refer to data in the graph when answering this question.

....

....

....

.... **(2 marks)**

Aseptic techniques

When answering several of the questions on this page, it is not enough to say 'it kills microorganisms'; you have to say why that is important.

1 Certain precautions must be taken when working with cultures of microorganisms. Draw **one** line from each precaution to a correct reason for it.

Precaution

| The workbench is wiped with disinfectant before starting work. |

| Petri dish lid is not completely sealed. |

| In school and college laboratories, cultures are incubated at 25 °C, not 37 °C. |

| The inoculating loop is sterilised before use. |

Reason

| To discourage the growth of anaerobic bacteria which are likely to be pathogens. |

| So that microorganisms on the bench do not contaminate the culture. |

| To prevent cross-contamination between cultures. |

| Pathogenic bacteria are more likely to grow at higher temperatures. |

(4 marks)

2 It is important that people doing experiments to culture microorganisms follow some safety precautions. For each precaution given, explain why it is important.

Guided

(a) The lid of the Petri dish is opened only enough to inoculate the agar plate.

This will .... microorganisms from the air that are

.... **(2 marks)**

(b) The inoculating loop is held in a flame before use.

....

.... **(2 marks)**

(c) The lid of the Petri dish is loosely taped down.

....

.... **(2 marks)**

3 A student is culturing some bacteria. Here are the steps he uses:
   • Agar jelly is heated to 80 °C.
   • The agar jelly is cooled and a sample of bacteria is added when the jelly is at 21 °C.
   • The jelly is put into sterilised Petri dishes and it is then warmed to 25 °C for around 6 hours.

State why each of these steps is important in making the bacterial culture safely and efficiently.

....

....

....

....

....

.... **(3 marks)**

Practical skills

Investigating microbial cultures

1 Paper discs were dipped into different antibiotics. They were placed on to a culture of bacteria, which was growing on nutrient agar in a Petri dish. The dish was then incubated for 3 days. The diagram shows the results.

bacterial growth
antibiotic disc

① ② ④ ③

(a) Explain why there are clear areas around each disc.

....

.... **(2 marks)**

(b) Complete the table by using the diagram.

Guided

Antibiotic	Diameter of clear area (mm)	Cross-sectional area (mm²)
1	7	$\pi(7/2)^2 = \pi \times 3.5^2 = 38.5$
2		
3		
4		

(4 marks)

(c) Which antibiotic is the most effective in this experiment? Explain your answer.

> Remember to use evidence from the experiment to justify your explanation.

....

....

.... **(2 marks)**

2 (a) Describe how the method in question 1 could be adapted to investigate the effect of concentration of antibiotic on growth of bacteria.

Guided

Use different concentrations of ....

....

....

.... **(3 marks)**

(b) State **two** ways in which you would make sure the investigation gives good results.

1. ....

....

2. ....

.... **(2 marks)**

New medicines

1 Development of a new medicine involves a series of stages. A new medicine can only move to the next stage if it has been successful in the previous stage.

(a) Complete the table to show the correct order of stages of developing a new drug.

Stage	Order
Testing in a small number of healthy people	
Discovery of possible new medicine	1
Given widely by doctors to treat patients	
Testing in cells or tissues in the lab	
Testing in a large number of people with the disease the medicine will treat	

(2 marks)

(b) (i) Describe **two** stages of preclinical testing in the development of a new medicine.

....

.... (2 marks)

(ii) Describe how development of a new medicine ensures that there are no dangerous side effects in humans.

.... (1 mark)

(c) Describe the function of a large clinical trial in developing a new drug.

For three marks you will have to describe all of the functions; pay attention to the word 'large'.

....

....

.... (3 marks)

2 Scientists trialled a new medicine that was developed to lower blood pressure. They took 1000 people with normal blood pressure (group A) and 1000 people with high blood pressure (group B). Each group was divided in half; half the volunteers were given the new medicine and the other half were given a placebo (dummy medicine). At the end of the trial, the scientists measured the number of volunteers in each group who had high blood pressure.

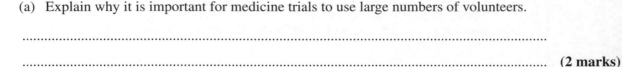

The results are shown in the bar chart.

(a) Explain why it is important for medicine trials to use large numbers of volunteers.

....

.... (2 marks)

(b) Use information from the bar chart to evaluate the effectiveness of this medicine.

....

.... (2 marks)

Non-communicable diseases

> Guided

1 Explain how an infectious disease is different to a non-communicable disease.

An infectious disease is caused by a .... and is passed from ....

.... A non-communicable disease

is not passed from .... **(3 marks)**

2 State **three** factors that can affect a person's risk of developing a non-communicable disease.

1. ....

2. ....

3. .... **(3 marks)**

3 The two graphs show the prevalence of coronary heart disease (CHD) in men and women from different ethnic groups in the West Midlands. Prevalence means the percentage of people in that ethnic group who are diagnosed with the disease.

(a) State the group with the:

   (i) highest incidence of CHD .... **(1 mark)**

   (ii) lowest incidence of CHD.. **(1 mark)**

(b) Discuss the effect of age, sex and ethnic group on the risk of developing CHD. Use the information in the graphs in your answer.

> **Discuss** means that you need to identify the issues being assessed by the question. You need to explore the different aspects of the issue – in this case, how the incidence of CHD varies with age, sex and ethnic group.

> Make sure that you cover all three factors (age, sex and ethnic group) as well as using data from the graph to support your conclusions.

....

....

....

....

....

.... **(4 marks)**

Alcohol and smoking

1 (a) Explain how alcohol (ethanol) causes liver disease.

....

....

....

....

....

.... **(3 marks)**

(b) State why alcohol-related liver disease is described as a lifestyle disease.

.... **(1 mark)**

2 Babies whose mothers smoked while pregnant have low birth weights. Explain why.

....

....

....

.... **(2 marks)**

3 (a) State **two** diseases caused by substances in cigarette smoke.

> The question asks you to state two diseases. Remember that heart attacks and strokes are not diseases, they are the result of disease.

....

.... **(2 marks)**

(b) A stroke is caused by cardiovascular disease in the brain. Explain how smoking can lead to a stroke.

Guided

Substances in cigarette smoke cause blood vessels to ....

....

....

....

.... **(3 marks)**

Malnutrition and obesity

1   The graph shows the percentage of different age groups with anaemia in a population in the USA during the 1990s.

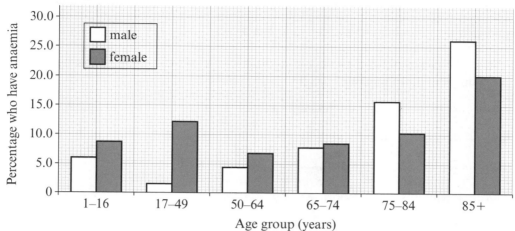

(a) Anaemia is a deficiency disease. State what is meant by deficiency disease.

.... **(1 mark)**

(b) Describe how the incidence of anaemia changes with age in males and females.

> Be sure to describe the trends in both males and females.

....

....

.... **(4 marks)**

> Guided

2   The table shows the height and mass of three people.

Subject	Mass (kg)	Height (m)	BMI
person A	80	1.80	$80/[(1.80)^2] = 80/3.24 = 24.7$
person B	90	1.65	
person C	95	2.00	

Complete the table by calculating the BMI for each person. **(2 marks)**

3   Measuring waist : hip ratio is better than BMI when predicting risk of cardiovascular disease.

(a) The table shows the waist and hip measurements of two men of the same age.

	Waist measurement (mm)	Hip measurement (m)	Waist : hip ratio
Man A	975	1.02	
Man B	914	1.06	

Complete the table by calculating the waist : hip ratio for each man. Give your answer to 2 decimal places. **(4 marks)**

(b) According to the World Health Organisation, men with a waist : hip ratio greater than 0.90 have an increased risk of developing cardiovascular disease.

Explain which man is more likely to develop cardiovascular disease.

....

.... **(2 marks)**

Cardiovascular disease

1 (a) State **two** ways in which cardiovascular disease may be treated.

....

.... **(2 marks)**

(b) State **two** pieces of advice a doctor might give to a patient with high blood pressure to help them make lifestyle changes.

....

....

.... **(2 marks)**

(c) Explain why it is more important to prevent cardiovascular disease than to treat it.

....

....

.... **(2 marks)**

2 The table summarises some of the benefits and drawbacks of the different types of treatment for cardiovascular disease.

Type of treatment	Benefits	Drawbacks
lifestyle changes	no side effects	may take time to work
medication	easier to do than change lifestyle	can have side effects
surgery		
		risk of infection after surgery

Complete the table with benefits and risks of the different types of treatment. **(3 marks)**

3 Angina is chest pain caused by narrowing of the coronary arteries. This can be treated using a stent. A stent is a wire frame that is inserted into the narrowed part of the artery. Angina can also be treated using heart bypass surgery. This is where the narrowed artery is bypassed using a section of artery or vein.

> Remember that the coronary arteries are in the heart and supply heart muscle. Think about the consequences if they become blocked.

Guided

Evaluate the use of surgery to treat angina.

Surgery can help prevent .... but costs more than inserting a

.... and surgery ....

However, ...

.... **(4 marks)**

 **Practical skills**

Plant defences

1 A student investigated whether garlic contains a substance that kills pathogens. She crushed some garlic in a little water to make a juice. She mixed this juice in a sterile tube with a bacterial culture and a nutrient-rich jelly. She put a lid on the top of the tube and left it for 2 days.

She repeated the investigation but used water rather than garlic juice.

> This question is about a practical piece of work. It is a good idea to look at your practical work before the exam to remind yourself of the skills you use when carrying out an experiment.

(a) State **two** ways in which plants protect themselves from pests and pathogens using physical barriers.

....

.... **(2 marks)**

(b) State **one** way in which plants use substances to protect themselves against pests and pathogens.

.... **(1 mark)**

(c) State the name of the part of the investigation that used water only.

.... **(1 mark)**

(d) Give **two** reasons why a lid was placed over the top of the tubes.

> **Guided**

To stop other ....

.... **(2 marks)**

(e) State **two** factors, other than those mentioned in the question, that should be kept constant in this investigation.

....

.... **(2 marks)**

(f) State an advantage to the garlic of containing an antibacterial substance.

.... **(1 mark)**

2 (a) State **two** different plant defences that may reduce the number of caterpillars on a plant.

....

.... **(2 marks)**

(b) Substances that plants produce for defence can be used as medicines. Aspirin, from the willow tree, is used to treat pain and fever. Give **two** ways that substances produced by plants for defence can be used as medicines.

....

.... **(2 marks)**

Extended response – Health and disease

Antibiotics and vaccines have become widely available. Their use has transformed the treatment of infectious diseases in the last hundred years.

Discuss the advantages and disadvantages of antibiotics and vaccines in the treatment of infectious diseases.

> You will be more successful in extended response questions if you plan your answer before you start writing.
>
> You don't need to draw a conclusion, but you do need to write a balanced account that covers both advantages and disadvantages of the two treatments.
>
> Don't be tempted to say too much about how each type of treatment works – focus on how effective they are at treating or preventing infectious diseases.

....

....

....

....

....

....

....

....

....

....

....

....

....

....

....

....

....

....

.... **(6 marks)**

Photosynthesis

1   Explain why it is that food chains start with plants or algae.

> Think about what a food chain represents. You will need to use terms such as producer and biomass in your answer.

....

....

.... **(3 marks)**

2   (a) Complete the equation to show the reactants and products of photosynthesis.

Guided   .... + water → .... + ...   **(2 marks)**

(b) Explain why photosynthesis is an endothermic reaction.

....

.... **(2 marks)**

3   A student knew that glucose, produced by photosynthesis, is converted into starch in leaves. She also knew that iodine solution turns blue–black in the presence of starch. The student carried out two experiments to investigate photosynthesis.

(a) The box shows what happened in the first experiment.

> **Experiment 1**
> A plant was kept in the dark for 48 hours. This removed all starch from its leaves. Some of the leaves were covered in foil. The plant was then placed on a sunny windowsill. Two leaves were tested for starch a few hours later:
> - the leaf covered in foil did not produce a blue-black colour with iodine;
> - the leaf left uncovered produced a blue-black colour with iodine.

Explain what Experiment 1 shows about photosynthesis.

....

.... **(2 marks)**

(b) In the second experiment, a plant with variegated leaves was used. Variegated leaves are green with white patches, rather than completely green.

> **Experiment 2**
> The plant was kept in the dark for 48 hours to remove all starch from its leaves. The plant was then placed on a sunny windowsill. A leaf was tested for starch a few hours later:
> - only the green parts of the leaf produced a blue-black colour with iodine.

Explain what Experiment 2 shows about photosynthesis.

> What is present in the green parts of the leaf that is not present in the white parts?

....

.... **(2 marks)**

Limiting factors

1 Describe what is meant by a limiting factor.

Guided

This is a factor or variable that stops the rate of something ....

The rate will only increase if this factor is .... **(2 marks)**

2 (a) Name **one** factor other than carbon dioxide concentration and light intensity that limits the rate of photosynthesis.

.... **(1 mark)**

(b) Describe how you could measure the rate of photosynthesis using algal balls.

....

....

....

....

.... **(3 marks)**

3 The graph shows how the rate of photosynthesis changes with light intensity. The data shows the rate at three different concentrations of carbon dioxide.

(a) Describe how increasing the concentration of carbon dioxide changes the rate of photosynthesis.

.... **(1 mark)**

(b) Commercial growers often increase the concentration of carbon dioxide in their greenhouses.

Explain how this will increase the yield of crops grown in the greenhouse.

....

.... **(2 marks)**

(c) Explain how the rate of photosynthesis could be increased further.

Guided

You could increase the .... as this

would make photosynthesis happen .... **(2 marks)**

 **Practical skills**

Light intensity

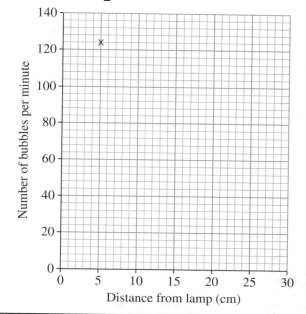

1   Some students wanted to investigate how the rate of photosynthesis in pond weed changed with light intensity. They did this by putting a lamp at different distances from some pond weed in a test tube. They counted the number of bubbles produced by the plant. Here is the data they collected.

Distance from lamp (cm)	5	10	15	20	25	30
Number of bubbles per minute	124	88	64	42	28	16

(a)   Complete the graph to show the results in the table. **(2 marks)**

> Mark the points accurately on the grid (to within half a square) using the table of data. Then draw a line of best fit through these points. This line does not have to be straight.

(b)   Use your graph to find the number of bubbles you would expect in 1 minute if the lamp was placed 12 cm from the pond weed.

.... **(1 mark)**

(c)   Describe how the rate of bubbling changes as the distance from the lamp increases.

....

.... **(2 marks)**

(d)   (i)   State **one** safety step you should take.

....

.... **(1 mark)**

(ii)   Explain **one** step you should take to ensure that your results are reliable.

> 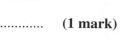 Explain means that you have to say what the step is and why you need to take that step.

....

....

.... **(2 marks)**

(e)   Describe how you could use a light meter to improve the experiment.

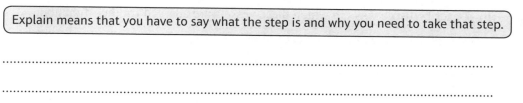 **Guided**   You could use the light meter to measure the .... at each

distance and then plot a graph of ....

.... **(2 marks)**

Specialised plant cells

1 The diagram shows part of a plant tissue specialised for transport.

(a) State the name of this type of tissue.

.... **(1 mark)**

A
mitochondrion
B
vacuole
companion cell
sieve cell

Guided

(b) Explain how the features labelled A and B are adapted to the function of this tissue.

A ....

....

B There is a small amount of cytoplasm so ....

.... **(4 marks)**

(c) Explain why companion cells have many mitochondria.

> Mitochondria supply energy. You need to give this information AND explain why companion cells need lots of energy.

....

....

.... **(2 marks)**

2 (a) State the name of the vessels used to transport water in plants.

.... **(1 mark)**

(b) Describe **three** ways in which these vessels are adapted for their function.

Guided

1. The walls are strengthened with lignin rings to..

....

2. ....

....

3. ....

.... **(3 marks)**

Transpiration

1 A student set up the following experiment to investigate transpiration.

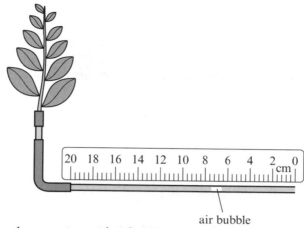

air bubble

(a) State what is meant by the term **transpiration**.

....

.... **(2 marks)**

(b) State which part of the plant regulates the rate of transpiration.

.... **(1 mark)**

(c) For each of the following situations, predict what will happen to the air bubble. Give a reason for each answer.

> The fan simulates a windy day.

(i) A fan is started in front of the plant.

....

.... **(2 marks)**

(ii) The undersides of the leaves of the plant are covered with grease.

....

.... **(2 marks)**

2 (a) Explain how the guard cells open and close.

....

....

....

.... **(3 marks)**

(b) The stomata are open during the day but closed at night. Explain why, in very hot weather, plants wilt during the day but recover during the night.

⟩ **Guided** ⟩

The stomata are open during the day, so water is lost by ....

faster than it can be absorbed by the .... Water is lost from the vacuoles

and the plant wilts. At night, the stomata ....

.... **(3 marks)**

Translocation

1 (a) State what is meant by translocation.

....

.... **(1 mark)**

(b) What is the name of the plant tissue responsible for translocation?

☐ **A** phloem

☐ **B** xylem

☐ **C** meristem

☐ **D** mesophyll   **(1 mark)**

2 (a) Describe how radioactive carbon dioxide can be used to show how sucrose is transported from a leaf to a storage organ such as a potato.

> **Guided**

Radioactive carbon dioxide is supplied to the leaf of a plant. ....

....

....

.... **(3 marks)**

(b) An inhibitor is a substance that can stop an enzyme or process working. Predict the effect on translocation of adding an inhibitor of active transport to the leaf. Give a reason for your answer.

> What type of transport is involved in translocation?

....

....

.... **(2 marks)**

3 The table lists some of the structures and mechanisms involved in movement of water and sucrose in the plant. Put an X in each row of the table to show whether the structure or mechanism is involved in the transport of water or sucrose.

> You might need to revise transpiration on page 53 of the Revision Guide before answering this question.

Structure or mechanism	Transport of water	Transport of sucrose
xylem		
phloem		
pulled by evaporation from the leaf		
requires energy		
transported up and down the plant		

(5 marks)

Leaf adaptations

1 The diagram shows a cross-section of part of the leaf of a plant.

(a) (i) State the name of the structure labelled A.

.... **(1 mark)**

(ii) Explain how structure A allows gas exchange while reducing water loss.

> Think about how the plant balances the need to allow entry of carbon dioxide while limiting loss of water.

....

....

.... **(2 marks)**

(b) Explain how the following are adapted to maximise the rate of photosynthesis:

(i) the epidermis

....

....

.... **(2 marks)**

(ii) the mesophyll cells

....

....

.... **(2 marks)**

(c) Explain the adaptation of the part of the leaf labelled B.

....

....

.... **(2 marks)**

2 Photosynthesis requires light energy, carbon dioxide and water to produce sugars.

(a) Explain why plants growing where there is not much light have large leaves.

Large leaves also have a large .... so they can

.... **(2 marks)**

(b) Describe how leaves are adapted to transport water and sugars.

....

....

.... **(2 marks)**

Water uptake in plants

1   The rate of transpiration increases if the light intensity or temperature is increased. Complete the table by placing a tick (✓) against information that could be used to explain this.

Information	Increased light intensity	Increased temperature
stomata become more open		
stomata become more closed		
water molecules have less energy		
water molecules have more energy		
rate of evaporation increased	✓	✓
rate of evaporation decreased		

(3 marks)

2   Some students investigated the rate at which water evaporated from leaves using this apparatus.

The students measured how far the air bubble travelled up the capillary tube in 5 minutes with the fan on, and with the fan off. They found that the bubble moved 90 mm with the fan off and 130 mm with the fan on.

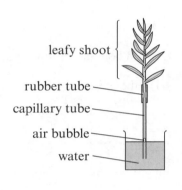

leafy shoot
rubber tube
capillary tube
air bubble
water

(a) Explain the results the students collected.

....

....

....

....   **(3 marks)**

(b) The speed of the fan was increased, and it was found that the rate that the bubble moved did not increase. Explain, in terms of the plant's response, why this was the case.

> In this question, you need to think about what the plant does as the speed of the wind increases.

....

....

....

....   **(3 marks)**

Guided

(c) The capillary tube had a diameter of 0.5 mm. Calculate the rate of transpiration in mm^3/min when the fan was off.

volume of tube = π × (diameter/2)^2 × length ....

= π × (...............)^2 × .... = ... mm^3

rate = volume/time = ... / .... mm^3/min

= .... mm^3/min (rounded to 1 decimal place)   **(2 marks)**

Plant adaptations

1   Many plants, such as roses, need to attract insects so that the plants can be pollinated and produce seeds.

(a)   Suggest how these plants are adapted in order to attract insects.

> **Guided**

Roses produce flowers to attract insects. These flowers have very bright

...., and they also give off a strong .... **(2 marks)**

(b)   The diagram shows the seeds that are produced by dandelions. Suggest how these seeds are adapted to make sure that they can be dispersed.

....

....

....

....   **(2 marks)**

2   The figure shows a leaf of philodendron, a common houseplant that grows wild in rainforests.

Explain **one** adaptation that philodendron has to help it grow in the rainforest.

....

.... **(2 marks)**

3   (a)   Pine trees grow in places where the water in the ground is frozen for several months of the year. Unlike deciduous trees, pine trees do not lose their needle-shaped leaves in the winter. Explain how the shape of their leaves allows pine trees to survive in winter without losing their leaves.

> Think about the effect on the tree if the water in the ground is frozen.

....

.... **(2 marks)**

(b)   The oleander is a shrub that grows in dry conditions around the Mediterranean. Explain how the following adaptations help oleander to survive:

(i)   a thick, waxy cuticle on the upper surface of the leaves

....

.... **(2 marks)**

(ii)   stomata that are sunken in deep pits lined with hairs

....

.... **(2 marks)**

Plant hormones

1   The diagram shows how a plant shoot responds to light.

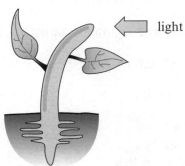

light

(a) Place an X on the diagram where auxins are produced.   **(1 mark)**

(b) Place a Y on the diagram to show where auxins travel causing the shoot to bend.   **(1 mark)**

(c) Place a Z on the part of the plant that shows positive gravitropism.   **(1 mark)**

2   (a) Explain why phototropism is important for shoots.

>**Guided**

Phototropism causes shoots to ....

This means that the leaves are positioned better to...

.... **(2 marks)**

(b) Explain why gravitropism is important for roots.

....

....

.... **(2 marks)**

3   The diagram shows a root emerging from a germinating seed.

(a) State the direction in which the root will grow. Give a reason for your answer.

> Include the stimulus to which the root responds in your answer.

....

.... **(2 marks)**

(b) Give **two** reasons why the response described in part (a) is important for roots.

1 ....

2 .... **(2 marks)**

(c) Explain how auxins affect the growth of the root.

....

....

.... **(3 marks)**

Extended response – Plant structures and functions

Plants need to exchange gases with their surroundings. Explain how gas exchange can lead to excess water loss from plants growing in very dry conditions. Explain how these plants may be adapted to help them survive.

> You will be more successful in extended response questions if you plan your answer before you start writing.
>
> This question is about water loss, so make sure that you explain how leaves are adapted for gas exchange and how this can lead to water loss.
>
> Then you can explain the adaptations of plants growing in very dry conditions. Make sure that you focus on adaptations that help plants survive in dry conditions.

....

....

....

....

....

....

....

....

....

....

....

....

....

....

....

....

....

....

....

....

....

.... **(6 marks)**

Hormones

1 (a) Describe how hormones behave like 'chemical messengers'.

Hormones are produced by .... and are released

into the .... They travel round the body until they reach

.... which responds by releasing

.... **(4 marks)**

(b) Describe **two** ways in which hormones and nerves communicate differently.

> Make sure you describe two ways and that they are differences, not similarities.

....

.... **(2 marks)**

2 The diagram shows the location of some endocrine glands in the body. Write in the name of each gland on the corresponding label line.

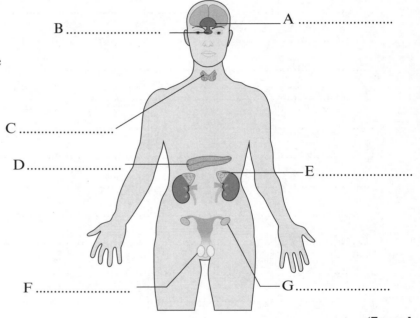

B ....

A ....

C ....

D.........................

E ....

F ....

G.........................

(7 marks)

3 Complete the table showing where some hormones are produced and where they have their action.

Hormone	Produced in	Site of action
thyroxine	thyroid gland	various organs, including the heart
FSH and LH		ovaries
insulin and glucagon		liver, muscle and adipose (fatty) tissue
adrenalin		various organs, e.g. heart, liver, skin
progesterone		uterus
testosterone		male reproductive organs

(5 marks)

The menstrual cycle

1 State **two** of the hormones that control the menstrual cycle.

.... **(2 marks)**

2 The diagram below shows the timing of some features in a menstrual cycle.

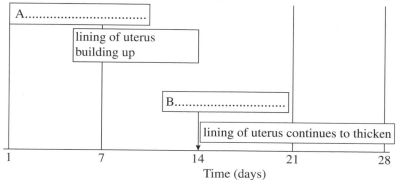

(a) Fill in the two missing labels, A and B, on the diagram.   **(2 marks)**

(b) Mark with an X on the diagram the point at which fertilisation is most likely to occur.   **(1 mark)**

(c) Describe what happens during days 1–5 of the cycle.

....

....

.... **(2 marks)**

3 (a) Explain how hormonal contraception prevents pregnancy.

> **Guided**

Pills, implants or injections release hormones that prevent ....

and thicken ....

preventing .... from passing.   **(3 marks)**

(b) The table shows the success rates of different methods of contraception.

Method of contraception	Success rate (% of pregnancies prevented)
hormonal pill or implant	> 99%
male condom	98%
diaphragm or cap	92 – 96%

(i) Explain why the actual success rate can sometimes be lower than the figures shown.

....

.... **(2 marks)**

(ii) Some methods of contraception protect against STIs as well as reducing the chance of pregnancy. Complete the table by placing a tick (✓) against the correct features of each method.

Method of contraception	Reduces chance of pregnancy (✓)	Protects against STIs (✓)
hormonal pill or implant		
male condom		
diaphragm or cap		

(3 marks)

Homeostasis

1 State what is meant by **homeostasis**.

....

....

.... **(2 marks)**

2 (a) State the location in the body of the thermoregulatory centre.

.... **(1 mark)**

(b) Explain why thermoregulation is important for the enzymes in the body.

....

....

.... **(2 marks)**

(c) Explain why we shiver if we don't wear enough clothes on a cold day.

Shivering means that energy is released from ....

which ....

.... **(2 marks)**

> **Guided**

3 (a) Explain what is meant by **osmoregulation**.

....

....

.... **(2 marks)**

(b) A student had heard that it was important to drink lots of water and so drank two 500 cm^3 bottles of water over a 30-minute period. The student found they had to urinate several times in the following 2 hours. Explain why the student's body had to get rid of water quickly.

....

....

.... **(2 marks)**

4 Predict what would happen to red blood cells if they were washed in water. Give a reason that explains your answer.

> Remember that osmosis is the net movement of water molecules across a partially permeable membrane, from a low solute concentration to a high solute concentration.

....

....

....

.... **(2 marks)**

Blood glucose regulation

1   The table shows the events that happen after a person eats a meal. Complete the table to show the order in which the events take place.

Guided

Event	Order
Pancreas increases secretion of insulin.	
Blood glucose concentration falls.	
Blood glucose concentration rises.	1
Insulin causes muscle and liver cells to remove glucose from blood and Store it as glycogen.	
Pancreas detects rise in blood glucose concentration.	

(3 marks)

2   The graph shows the effect of a hormone on the concentration of glucose in the blood.

(a)   Calculate the percentage change in blood glucose concentration after eating dinner.   **(2 marks)**

> Remember that you can draw lines on the graph if this helps you to work out your answer.

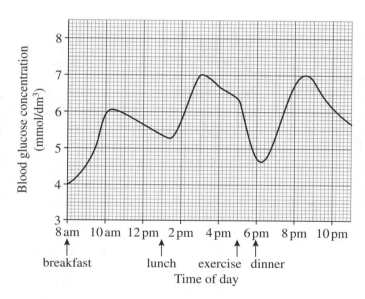

(b)   Explain why there is a decrease in blood glucose concentration between 10 am and 1 pm.

....

.... **(2 marks)**

(c)   Explain why the blood glucose concentration decreases more rapidly between 5 pm and 6 pm.

....

....

.... **(2 marks)**

Diabetes

1 (a) The graph shows the percentage of people in one area of the USA in the year 2000 who have Type 2 diabetes, divided into groups according to body mass index.

Describe how the percentage of people with Type 2 diabetes changes as the BMI increases.

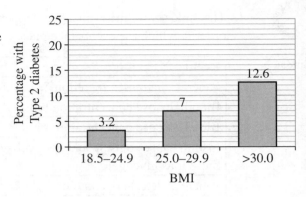

....

.... **(2 marks)**

   (b) Two 45-year-old males from the area of the USA studied in part (a) wanted to estimate their chances of developing Type 2 diabetes.

   (i) George was 180 cm tall and had a mass of 88 kg. Calculate his BMI and use this to evaluate his risk of developing Type 2 diabetes.

$$BMI = \frac{weight\ (kg)}{(height\ (m))^2}$$

.... **(3 marks)**

   (ii) Donald had a waist measurement of 104 cm and a hip measurement of 102 cm. The World Health Organization classes a waist : hip ratio of >0.9 as obese. State and explain whether Donald has an increased risk of developing Type 2 diabetes.

....

....

.... **(3 marks)**

2 (a) Explain how helping people to control their diets might help to reduce the percentage of people in the population who have diabetes.

Guided

Controlling diets will help to..

Fewer obese people means.. **(2 marks)**

   (b) (i) Explain why people with Type 1 diabetes are treated with insulin but most people with Type 2 diabetes are not.

....

.... **(2 marks)**

   (ii) Explain why a person with Type 1 diabetes will sometimes wait to see how large a meal is before deciding how much insulin to inject.

....

.... **(2 marks)**

The urinary system

1 The diagram shows the human urinary system.

(a) Label structures A – F on the diagram. Choose from the words in the box.

bladder	kidney	urethra
ureter	renal artery	renal vein

(3 marks)

blood towards the heart

blood towards the kidney

B ....

A ....

C ....

D ....

E ....

muscle

F ....

(b) (i) State the name of the main waste substance that is removed from the blood.

.... **(1 mark)**

(ii) State where in the body this substance is produced.

.... **(1 mark)**

> Make sure that you know the difference between urea and urine, and between ureter and urethra.

(c) Describe the function of the following structures:

Guided

A: removes .... and makes ....

B: ....

D: ....

muscle: .... **(4 marks)**

2 The table shows the concentration of some substances in the blood, filtration fluid and urine.

Substance	Concentration ($g\,dm^{-3}$)		
	Blood	**Filtration fluid**	**Urine**
water	900.0	900.0	900.0
proteins	80.0	0.0	0.0
glucose	1.0	1.0	0.0
urea	0.3	0.3	20.0
sodium ions	3.0	3.0	5.0

> Remember that **explain** means that you need a statement and a reason.

(a) Explain the differences in the concentration of the following:

(i) proteins ....

.... **(2 marks)**

(ii) glucose ....

.... **(2 marks)**

(iii) urea ....

....

.... **(3 marks)**

(b) Explain why the concentrations of water and sodium ions in urine are sometimes different to the values shown in the table.

....

....

.... **(2 marks)**

Kidney treatments

1 (a) Explain why a person with kidney failure will have to receive kidney dialysis every few days.

> Although you need to be able to describe only treatments for kidney failure, you may have to use earlier knowledge to answer a question like this.

....

.... **(2 marks)**

(b) Describe the function of the partially permeable membrane in a kidney dialysis machine.

....

.... **(2 marks)**

(c) The table compares the concentrations of some substances during kidney dialysis.

Guided

	A	B	Comparison
Concentration of glucose in:	dialysis fluid at start of dialysis	blood at start of dialysis	same
Concentration of glucose in:	dialysis fluid at end of dialysis	blood at end of dialysis	
Concentration of urea in:	dialysis fluid at start of dialysis	blood at start of dialysis	
Concentration of urea in:	blood at start of dialysis	blood at end of dialysis	

Complete the table by writing in whether concentration A or B is higher or if they are the same. **(4 marks)**

(d) Explain why it is necessary to keep the dialysis fluid flowing through the machine during kidney dialysis.

....

.... **(2 marks)**

2 Kidney failure often happens as a result of diabetes. What would happen to the concentration of glucose in the blood of a person with diabetes during kidney dialysis? Give a reason for your answer.

....

.... **(2 marks)**

3 Organ transplantation is a better treatment for most people with kidney failure.

(a) Describe how a kidney transplantation is carried out.

....

.... **(2 marks)**

(b) It is more difficult to find a suitable donor for some patients. Suggest a reason that explains why this is.

.... **(1 mark)**

Extended response – Control and coordination

 Compare how Type 1 and Type 2 diabetes are caused and how they are treated.

> You will be more successful in extended response questions if you plan your answer before you start writing.
>
> Make sure that you cover the causes of each type of diabetes and link this to the type of treatment.

....

....

....

....

....

....

....

....

....

....

....

....

....

....

....

....

....

....

....

....

....

....

.... **(6 marks)**

Exchanging materials

1 Substances are transported into and out of the body. Describe where and why the following substances are removed from the bloodstream.

(a) Water ....

....

.... **(2 marks)**

(b) Urea ....

....

.... **(2 marks)**

2 Humans and other mammals need to exchange gases with their environment. Describe where and why this exchange happens.

....

....

.... **(3 marks)**

3 Absorption of digested food molecules takes place in the small intestine. The small intestine has a surface adapted to assist this process.

Guided

(a) Describe how the small intestine is adapted to help to absorb food molecules.

The surface of the small intestine is covered with .... These help

by increasing ....

.... **(2 marks)**

(b) Explain why the structures described in part (a) have thin walls.

....

.... **(2 marks)**

4 The diagram shows a flatworm and an earthworm.

Guided

The two worms are similar in size. Explain why the flatworm does not have an exchange system or a transport system whereas the earthworm has a transport system (heart and blood vessels).

The flatworm is very flat and thin which means it has a large ....

....

....

....

.... **(4 marks)**

Alveoli

1 (a) Describe how gas exchange takes place in the lungs.

Oxygen diffuses from .... into ....

Carbon dioxide diffuses from .... into .... **(2 marks)**

(b) State and explain **two** ways in which the structure of the alveoli is adapted for efficient gas exchange.

Millions of alveoli create a large ....

for the .... of gases. Each alveolus is closely associated with

a .... Their walls are one ....

.... **(4 marks)**

2 Explain the importance of continual breathing and blood flow for gas exchange.

....

....

....

.... **(2 marks)**

3 Emphysema is a type of lung disease where elastic tissue in the alveoli breaks down. The figure shows the appearance of an alveolus damaged by lung disease compared with a healthy alveolus.

> Think about what effects the changes seen in emphysema would have on gas exchange and how this would then affect the person.

Healthy alveolus   Alveolus damaged by lung disease

Explain how emphysema affects the person.

....

....

....

....

....

.... **(3 marks)**

Rate of diffusion

1 Lungs are an exchange surface that allow gases to be exchanged between the blood and air.

(a) Describe **three** factors that increase the effectiveness of the lungs as an exchange surface.

....

....

.... **(3 marks)**

(b) For each factor you have mentioned in part (a), describe **one** way in which the lungs are adapted to increase their effectiveness as an exchange surface.

> Make sure that you link each example to each factor you have mentioned.

....

....

.... **(3 marks)**

2 Fick's law can be used to calculate the rate of diffusion across an exchange surface.

(a) Pulmonary fibrosis is caused by damage to the alveoli. It leads to thick scar tissue forming in the lungs. The scar tissue in a person with pulmonary fibrosis has increased the thickness of the membranes in the lungs by a factor of 3. Use Fick's law to describe what would happen to the rate of gas diffusion in this person.

> Fick's law is: rate of diffusion $\propto \dfrac{\text{surface area} \times \text{concentration difference}}{\text{thickness of membrane}}$

....

....

.... **(2 marks)**

(b) Explain what symptoms you would expect in a person with pulmonary fibrosis.

....

....

.... **(2 marks)**

⟩Guided⟩ (c) Coronary heart disease reduces the flow of blood through the lungs. Explain why patients with coronary heart disease have similar symptoms to those you have described in your answer to part (b).

Reduced blood flow would reduce the ....

in the .... and so less ....

.... **(2 marks)**

Blood

1 Draw **one** line from each blood component to a correct function.

Blood component		Function
plasma		carries other blood components
platelet		part of the body's immune system
red blood cell		involved in forming blood clots
white blood cell		carries oxygen

(4 marks)

2 Blood contains red blood cells.

(a) Name the cell structure, normally found in cells, that is missing in human red blood cells.

.... (1 mark)

(b) Name the compound in red blood cells that gives them their colour.

.... (1 mark)

(c) The diagram shows some red blood cells.

Describe **two** ways in which red blood cells are adapted to carry out their function.

Their biconcave shape gives them a large ....

for diffusion to happen efficiently. They are also flexible, which lets them

.... (2 marks)

3 The plasma transports soluble products of digestion, including glucose and amino acids. Name **two** waste substances transported by the plasma.

1 ....

2 .... (2 marks)

4 Explain how platelets help to protect the body from infection.

....

....

.... (3 marks)

5 White blood cells usually make up about 1% of the blood and include lymphocytes and phagocytes.

(a) Explain why the number of lymphocytes increases during infection.

....

....

.... (3 marks)

(b) Describe how phagocytes help protect the body.

....

.... (2 marks)

Blood vessels

Guided

1 (a) Describe the structure of an artery.

An artery has .... walls. These walls are composed of two types of fibres:

.... tissue and .... fibres.   **(3 marks)**

(b) Explain how the structure of the artery wall makes blood flow more smoothly in arteries.

....

....

....   **(2 marks)**

2 Blood needs to penetrate every organ in the body. This is made possible by capillaries.

(a) Describe how the capillaries are adapted for this function.

> Make sure that you describe here and save the explanation for part (b).

....

....

....   **(2 marks)**

(b) Explain how the features you have described are important for the function of capillaries.

....

....

....   **(2 marks)**

3 (a) Veins carry blood away from the organs of the body to the heart.

(i) Explain why there is a difference in the thickness of the walls of arteries and veins.

....

....

....   **(2 marks)**

(ii) Explain how muscles and valves work together to help return blood to the heart.

....

....

....   **(2 marks)**

(b) Explain why a nurse taking blood from a patient will insert a needle into a vein rather than an artery.

> There are two possible answers here – you need to consider either the structure of the different blood vessels, or else the way in which each transports the blood they contain.

....

....

....   **(2 marks)**

The heart

Guided ▷

1 The heart is connected to four major blood vessels. Describe where each vessel carries blood.

Blood vessel	Carries blood:	
	from	to
aorta	heart	body
pulmonary artery		
pulmonary vein		
vena cava		

(4 marks)

2 (a) Explain why the heart consists mostly of muscle.

....

.... **(2 marks)**

(b) Describe the route taken by blood through the heart from the vena cava to the aorta.

....

....

.... **(3 marks)**

3 The diagram shows a section through the human heart.

> Remember that the heart is drawn and labelled as if you were looking at the heart in someone's body. So the right side of the heart is actually on the left side of the page!

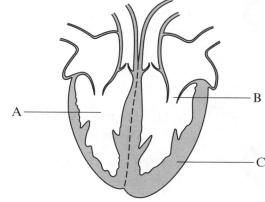

(a) State the name of the part of the heart labelled A and describe its function.

....

.... **(2 marks)**

(b) Explain the function of the part labelled B.

....

.... **(2 marks)**

(c) Explain why the muscle at C needs to be thicker than on the other side of the heart.

....

....

.... **(3 marks)**

Aerobic respiration

1 Read the following passage and answer the questions that follow.

> Aerobic respiration happens in muscle cells in the body. The muscle cells are surrounded by blood vessels. The substances needed for respiration are transferred to the muscle cells by diffusion, and the waste products are removed.

(a) Name the substances needed for respiration in muscle cells.

.... and .... **(2 marks)**

(b) State the meaning of the term **diffusion**.

Guided

Diffusion is the movement of substances from .... to ....
concentration. **(1 mark)**

2 (a) State the location in the cell where most of the reactions of aerobic respiration occur.

.... **(1 mark)**

(b) Explain how cellular respiration helps maintain the body temperature.

....

....

.... **(2 marks)**

(c) State **one** way that animals use energy from respiration, other than to maintain their body temperature.

....

.... **(1 mark)**

3 The blood supplies cells with the substances needed for aerobic respiration, as well as removing waste products.

(a) Write a word equation for aerobic respiration.

.... **(1 mark)**

(b) State the name of the smallest blood vessels that carry blood to the respiring cells.

.... **(1 mark)**

4 (a) Explain why all organisms respire continuously.

....

.... **(2 marks)**

(b) Plants can use energy from sunlight in photosynthesis. Explain why plants also need to respire continuously.

> Photosynthesis uses light energy in production of glucose; it does not release energy that can be used in other processes. Think about why plants need energy from respiration.

....

.... **(2 marks)**

Anaerobic respiration

1 Humans can respire in two ways: using oxygen (aerobic) and without using oxygen (anaerobic).

> Make sure that you understand what is produced in both aerobic and anaerobic respiration.

(a) Compare the amounts of energy transferred by aerobic and anaerobic respiration.

....

.... **(2 marks)**

(b) Describe the circumstances under which anaerobic respiration occurs.

....

.... **(2 marks)**

2 In track cycling, a 'sprint' event begins with several slow laps in which the riders try to get a tactical advantage. These slow laps are followed by a very fast sprint to the finishing line.

(a) Describe and explain how the cyclists' heart rates change during the course of the race.

....

....

.... **(3 marks)**

(b) After the race the cyclists will cycle on a stationary bicycle for 5–10 minutes. Explain why they do this.

....

.... **(2 marks)**

3 The graph shows how oxygen consumption changes before, during and after exercise. The intensity of the exercise kept increasing during the period marked 'Exercise'.

(a) Explain the shape of the graph during the period marked 'Exercise'.

....

....

.... **(3 marks)**

> Guided

(b) Explain the shape of the graph during the period marked 'Recovery'.

During exercise there is an increase in the concentration of ....

....

....

.... **(2 marks)**

Rate of respiration

1   The diagram shows a respirometer used to investigate the rate of respiration in germinating peas.

> This is one of the core practicals so you should be able to answer questions on the apparatus.

syringe containing air

3-way tap

ruler

capillary tubing

blob of liquid

respiring peas

wire gauze

water bath

potassium hydroxide

State the role of the following and give a reason for your answer:

(a) the water bath

....

....

.... **(2 marks)**

> **Guided**

(b) the potassium hydroxide

Absorbs carbon dioxide produced by the .... so that

....

.... **(2 marks)**

(c) the tap and syringe containing air

....

....

.... **(2 marks)**

2   (a) Explain how the apparatus allows you to measure the rate of respiration in the seeds.

> The movement of the liquid blob gives you information about the uptake of oxygen. You need to state this, explain how you measure the movement and then how you calculate the rate of respiration.

....

....

.... **(3 marks)**

(b) Describe how you would use the apparatus to investigate the effect of temperature on the rate of respiration in peas.

....

....

.... **(3 marks)**

Changes in heart rate

1 Cardiac output can be calculated using the equation:
cardiac output = stroke volume × heart rate.

(a) What is meant by the term **stroke volume**?

.... **(1 mark)**

(b) A man has an average stroke volume of $75 \, cm^3$ and a heart rate of 60 beats/minute.

   (i) Calculate his cardiac output. Show your working out and give the correct units.

Cardiac output .... **(3 marks)**

   (ii) Explain the change in cardiac output when the man starts to exercise.

....

....

.... **(3 marks)**

2 The graph shows the pulse rate of an athlete at rest, and after 5 minutes of different types of exercise.

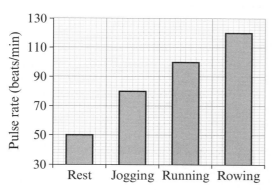

Remember to show all your steps in the calculation.

(a) Calculate the percentage increase in pulse rate between jogging and running.

100 beats/min – 80 beats/min = .../min

(............/80) × 100 =

Percentage increase .... **(2 marks)**

(b) State why the pulse rate is highest when the athlete is rowing.

....

.... **(1 mark)**

(c) The pulse is a measure of heart rate. At rest, the cardiac output of the athlete is $4000 \, cm^3$/min. Calculate the stroke volume, in cm^3, of the athlete at rest.

Stroke volume .... cm^3 **(2 marks)**

Extended response – Exchange

The diagram shows the main features of the human heart and circulatory system.

Describe the journey taken by blood around the body and through the heart, starting from when it enters the right side of the heart. In your answer, include names of major blood vessels and chambers in the heart.

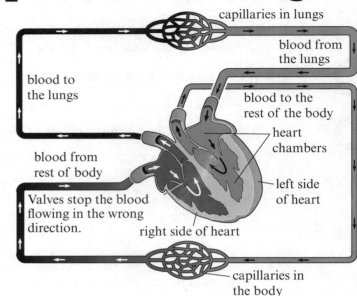

capillaries in lungs

blood from the lungs

blood to the lungs

blood to the rest of the body

heart chambers

left side of heart

blood from rest of body

Valves stop the blood flowing in the wrong direction.

right side of heart

capillaries in the body

> You will be more successful with extended response questions if you plan your answer before you start writing.
>
> You do not need to explain how the different components of the heart and circulatory system work. It may help your plan if you follow the blood around the diagram with a finger, writing the name of each blood vessel or chamber in order as you go. You do not need to identify any blood vessels in the 'rest of the body' other than the aorta.

....

....

....

....

....

....

....

....

....

....

....

....

....

....

....

.... **(6 marks)**

Ecosystems and abiotic factors

1 Draw lines to connect each term with its definition.

Term	Definition
Community	A single living individual
Organism	All the living organisms and the non-living components in an area
Population	All the populations in an area
Ecosystem	All the organisms of the same species in an area

(4 marks)

2 A student surveyed the distribution of a species of lichen growing on the trunk of a tree. She used a small quadrat to measure the percentage cover by these lichens on the south- and north-facing sides of the tree.

	Light intensity (lux)			
	Reading 1	Reading 2	Reading 3	Mean
South side	275.5	368.1	326.8	
North side	195.7	282.1	205.1	

Percentage cover											
South side						North side					
1	2	3	4	5	Mean	1	2	3	4	5	Mean
48	20	28	92	8	39	4	4	4	4	6	4

(a) Complete the upper table to show the mean light intensity for each side.

> **Guided**

south side $\dfrac{(275.5 + 368.1 + 326.8)}{3} =$

north side .... **(2 marks)**

(b) The student concluded that the lichen was better adapted to conditions on the south side. Justify her conclusions.

> In this part of the question you are asked to say only whether she was right and, if so, why. Don't try to explain her results.

....

....

....

.... **(2 marks)**

(c) Light intensity is an abiotic factor. Explain one other abiotic factor that might be responsible for the different distribution of lichen.

....

....

....

.... **(2 marks)**

Biotic factors

1   Meerkats are animals that live in packs and are found in the desert areas of southern Africa. The pack of meerkats is led by a dominant pair of meerkats, known as the alpha male and female.

> In this question, you will be asked to think about aspects of the behaviour of the meerkats. Remember to link your answer to the ideas that these animals will compete with each other for resources.

(a)   State what the term **biotic factors** means.

....   **(1 mark)**

(b)   Only the alpha male and alpha female breed. Suggest an explanation for why younger male meerkats will often try to fight the alpha male.

....

....   **(2 marks)**

(c)   When meerkat packs become very large, they often split into smaller packs. The new pack will often move some distance from the original pack. Explain the reasons why a large pack may need to split up.

> Make sure that you know what the command words mean. **Explain** means give a reason why. **Suggest** means that you need to apply your knowledge to a new situation. **Describe** means say what is happening.

....

....   **(2 marks)**

2   The drawing shows a male peacock.

State and explain **one** adaptation, seen in the diagram, that helps the peacock attract a mate.

....

....

....

....   **(3 marks)**

3   The diagram shows a cross-section through a tropical rainforest.

> **Guided**

(a)   Some trees are called emergent. They break through the rest of the rainforest canopy. Explain the advantage to these trees of emerging from the canopy.

The trees emerge through the canopy

to get .... for

more .... **(2 marks)**

(b)   The soil in a rainforest is often poor as the minerals are washed away (leached). Suggest an explanation of how trees in the rainforest may adapt in response to a leached soil.

....

....   **(2 marks)**

emergent
layer

canopy
layer

Parasitism and mutualism

1   The table has statements about relationships between species. Place an X in one of the boxes on each line to show whether the statement applies to parasitism only, mutualism only, or both parasitism and mutualism.

Statement	Parasitism only	Mutualism only	Both parasitism and mutualism
There is interdependence, where the survival of one species is closely linked with another species.			
One species lives inside the intestine of another and absorbs nutrients from the digested food.			
One species lives inside another and receives food from the host. In return, the host receives nutrients.			

(3 marks)

2   Cleaner fish are small fish that feed on parasites on the skin of sharks. Describe how the cleaner fish and the sharks benefit from a mutualistic relationship.

> **Guided**

Cleaner fish get food by...

....

This helps the shark because ....

.... (2 marks)

> An exam question may ask you about the benefits to one organism or to both. Make sure that you read the question carefully!

3   The scabies mite is a tiny arthropod that burrows into human skin and lays its eggs. Infection by the scabies mite causes severe itching and a lumpy, red rash that can appear anywhere on the body. Explain why the scabies mite is a parasite and not a mutualist.

> This type of question is expecting you to apply your understanding of science to a situation that you may not be familiar with. You will have been taught about organisms that behave in a similar way to the scabies mite – use what you know about these organisms but apply it to the scabies mite.

....

....

....

.... (2 marks)

Fieldwork techniques

1 A gardener goes into his garden every night at 7 pm and counts the number of slugs in the same 1 m² area of his flower bed. He records his results in a table.

Day	Monday	Tuesday	Wednesday	Thursday	Friday	Saturday	Sunday
Number of slugs	11	12	7	12	8	8	12

(a) Describe how the gardener could make sure the 1 m² area of the flower bed was chosen at random on the first day.

....

.... **(2 marks)**

> **Guided**

(b) Why does the gardener use the same area each time?

Using the same area means that his experiment is .... **(1 mark)**

(c) Describe **one** way in which the gardener could improve the repeatability of the data that he collected.

....

.... **(2 marks)**

2 A class is investigating the number of clover plants on a football pitch. The pitch measures 100 m by 65 m. The class wants to find the total number of clover plants in the field. The teacher gives the class a 1 m × 1 m quadrat.

> mean number of plants = $\dfrac{\text{total number of plants in all quadrats}}{\text{number of quadrats}}$

(a) Explain how the class can use the quadrat to estimate the mean number of clover plants in a 1 m² area.

....

.... **(2 marks)**

(b) The class finds that the mean number of clover plants in an area of 1 m × 1 m is 7. Estimate the number of clover plants on the whole football pitch.

....

....

.... **(3 marks)**

3 Describe how you would use a belt transect to investigate the distribution of broad-leaved plants growing alongside a path that started at a road, crossed a small field and entered a wood.

> Make sure that you describe use of quadrats, the measurements you would take and what you would record.

....

....

....

.... **(3 marks)**

Organisms and their environment

1 Limpets are animals that have a shell and live on rocks that are underwater some or all of the time. They can be found in the sea, or in rock pools on the beach. A scientist is investigating the distribution of limpets on the beach.

   (a) Explain how the scientist could use a transect to investigate the distribution of limpets.

   ....

   ....

   ....   **(3 marks)**

The scientist sets up three different transects and measures the numbers of limpets on each one. His data are shown in the table.

Distance from sea (metres)	Number of limpets			Mean number of limpets
	Transect 1	Transect 2	Transect 3	
0.5	20	23	20	21
1.0	18	16	17	17
1.5	13	13	13	13
2.0	10	8	9	
2.5	5	6	4	5

   (b) Calculate the mean number of limpets at 2.0 m from the sea in this investigation.

   ....   **(2 marks)**

   (c) What conclusion can be made from his investigation?

   > Your conclusion should describe how the distribution of limpets changes along the transect.

   ....

   ....

   ....   **(3 marks)**

2 A scientist investigated the distribution of bluebells in a large wood. She started on the edge of the wood, and measured a line going deeper into the wood. Every 2 m into the woodland, she placed a quadrat and counted the number of bluebells in the quadrat. She also measured the light intensity at each quadrat.

   (a) Describe **one** way the scientist could alter her method to collect more accurate data.

   Instead of placing a quadrat every 2 m, the scientist could ....

   .... and use a .... quadrat than before. **(2 marks)**

   (b) The scientist obtained the following data:

Distance from edge of wood in metres	0	2	4	6	8	10	12	14	16
Number of bluebells	0	7	15	22	25	21	16	10	8

   Suggest an explanation for these results.

   ....

   ....   **(2 marks)**

Guided

97

Energy transfer between trophic levels

1 The diagram shows a food web.

(a) Identify the producer in this food web.

....

(1 mark)

(b) State the number of trophic levels in this food web.

....

(1 mark)

(c) Explain why it is unusual to have more than this number of trophic levels.

Because there is not enough biomass in the

top level ....

.... **(2 marks)**

owls

snakes

stoats

grasshoppers   mice   rabbits

grass

2 The table gives details about the trophic levels in a food chain.

(a) Calculate the biomass at each trophic level. Write your answers in the spaces in the table.

Organism	Energy at each trophic level (J)	Number of organisms	Mass of each organism (kg)	Biomass at each trophic level (kg)
Producers	7550	10 000	0.25	10 000 × 0.25 = 2500
Herbivores	640	200	2.5	
Carnivores	53	10	20	

(1 mark)

(b) Use your calculations to draw a pyramid of biomass for the food chain shown in the table.

> If you are asked to draw a pyramid of biomass, make sure you draw it to scale.
>
> Here, 1 mm = 25 organisms works.

(2 marks)

(c) Calculate the percentage of energy that is transferred from the herbivores to the carnivores.

percentage of energy .... **(2 marks)**

(d) Explain why the amount of energy decreases as it is transferred from one trophic level to the next.

....

.... **(2 marks)**

Human effects on ecosystems

Guided

1   Fish can be farmed or caught from the wild. State **one** advantage of fish farming, and **one** disadvantage.

Advantage reduces fishing of ....

Disadvantage ....

.... **(2 marks)**

2   A non-indigenous species is not naturally found in a particular place. For example, the cane toad is a non-indigenous species in Australia that was introduced to control insect pests. State **one** other advantage of introducing a non-indigenous species, and **one** disadvantage.

Advantage ....

....

Guided

Disadvantage may reproduce rapidly as they ....

....

.... **(2 marks)**

3   The graph shows the mass of fertiliser used in the world from 1950 to 2003.

(a)   Calculate the percentage increase in fertiliser use from 1950 to 2003.

> Make sure that you read the graph carefully to get the correct figures for your calculation. You will get one mark for showing the correct calculation and one mark for the correct answer.

.... **(2 marks)**

(b)   Suggest an explanation for the change in the mass of fertiliser used worldwide since 1950.

....

....

.... **(2 marks)**

(c)   Describe an environmental problem caused by over-use of fertilisers.

....

.... **(2 marks)**

Biodiversity

1 (a) State what is meant by reforestation.

....

.... **(1 mark)**

(b) Describe **two** advantages of reforestation.

....

....

....

.... **(2 marks)**

2 Explain the importance to humans of conservation.

....

....

....

.... **(2 marks)**

3 Yellowstone National Park in the USA is the natural home of many species. Deer eat young trees, stopping them from growing. The population of deer increased so much that Park authorities decided to reintroduce some wolves.

The wolves killed some of the deer for food. The deer moved away from river areas because they were more easily hunted by the wolves there. The wolves also killed coyotes, which are predators that eat rabbits.

The reintroduction of wolves led to major improvements in the biodiversity of the Park. This included increases in the populations of rabbits, bears, hawks and other birds. It also reduced the amount of soil washed into the rivers.

Describe the ways in which the reintroduction of the wolves may have caused the biodiversity to improve.

> This is an example of having to apply knowledge you have learned in this and other units to an unfamiliar situation.

The numbers of trees will increase because ....

This means there will be more food for ....

There will be more rabbits because ....

If there are more rabbits, there will be more food for . ...

More trees also mean ....

.... **(5 marks)**

Food security

1 (a) State what is meant by food security.

.... **(1 mark)**

(b) Explain why increasing human populations increase the need for food security.

> This is not just about the numbers, it is also about living standards.

....

....

.... **(2 marks)**

(c) State what is meant by sustainability.

....

....

.... **(2 marks)**

2 Growing soya to produce biodiesel (a biofuel) can help to reduce use of fossil fuels.

(a) Explain what effect this might have on the food supply for human populations.

....

.... **(2 marks)**

(b) Describe **two** ways in which biodiesel production may not be sustainable.

....

....

.... **(2 marks)**

3 Some people think that intensive farming methods will help to meet growing demand for meat. However, it takes about 7 kg of feed (produced from grain) to produce 1 kg of beef.

> Guided

Explain why some people think the use of intensive farming may not improve food security in a sustainable way.

7 kg of grain will feed more people than 1 kg of beef ....

....

....

....

....

.... **(3 marks)**

The carbon cycle

1 Complete the diagram of the carbon cycle by writing the names of the processes in the boxes.

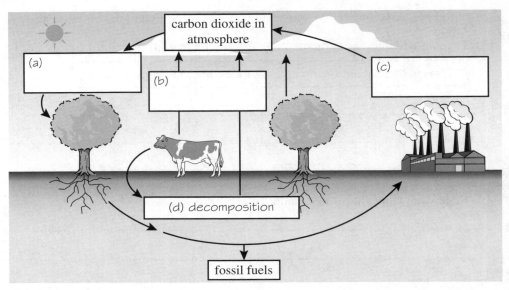

carbon dioxide in atmosphere

(a)

(b)

(c)

(d) decomposition

fossil fuels

(4 marks)

2 Explain why microorganisms are important in recycling carbon in the environment.

....

....

.... **(2 marks)**

> In questions about the carbon cycle, you will be expected to make links between photosynthesis, respiration and combustion, and the amount of carbon dioxide in the air.

3 (a) The diagram shows a fish tank. Explain how carbon is recycled between organisms in the fish tank.

....

....

....

....

....

....

.... **(4 marks)**

   (b) Explain why it is important that numbers of both plant and animal populations in the fish tank are kept balanced.

....

....

.... **(3 marks)**

The water cycle

1 (a) Give **three** natural sources of water vapour in the atmosphere.

> The question says 'water vapour' so make sure that your answer talks about the formation of water vapour and not about other aspects of the water cycle.

....

....

....

....

.... **(3 marks)**

(b) Describe what happens when water vapour in the atmosphere condenses.

....

....

....

....

.... **(3 marks)**

2 In parts of California there is a lack of rainfall. Water has been taken from rivers and used to water lawns and golf courses. Some of these areas are suffering from drought and there are now restrictions on the number of days a week golf courses can be watered. Explain why these restrictions have been introduced.

> Guided

A lot of water evaporates from golf courses so this will lead to...............................

....

....

.... **(3 marks)**

3 Sea water contains too much salt to make it potable (safe to drink). Potable water can be produced from sea water by desalination:

• sea water is evaporated by heating

• water vapour is cooled and condensed.

Give **one** advantage of desalination to people in areas where there is a drought, and **one** disadvantage.

....

....

....

.... **(2 marks)**

The nitrogen cycle

The diagram shows how the element nitrogen moves between living organisms and the environment.

1 Bacteria are involved in different stages of the nitrogen cycle. Which is the correct combination of processes involving bacteria?

☐ **A** processes A and B only

☐ **B** processes A, B and C only

☐ **C** processes A, B, C and D only

☐ **D** processes A, B, C, D and E   **(1 mark)**

A Nitrogen fixation in root nodules
B Nitrogen fixation in soil
C Denitrification
D Decomposition
E Absorption

2 (a) Describe the process happening in B.

> **Guided**

Nitrogen fixation by .... **(1 mark)**

(b) Explain the importance of process E.

....

....

....

....

.... **(3 marks)**

(c) Explain the importance of bacteria in stage C.

....

....

....

.... **(2 marks)**

3 Some farmers use crop rotation, with different crops each year, including a 'green manure' crop such as clover.

Explain the importance of process A in crop rotation.

> You need to say something about how clover is involved in process A as well as its importance for crop plants.

....

....

....

....

.... **(3 marks)**

Decay

1 A gardener uses compost in the soil of his garden. The gardener makes the compost himself. He then grows tomatoes in the soil.

> Guided

(a) The compost is made from garden waste. What conditions are needed for compost to form from the garden waste?

The conditions needed are oxygen, ...

and .... **(3 marks)**

(b) Explain why the gardener puts the heap in a sunny part of the garden.

....

....

.... **(2 marks)**

(c) Explain why the gardener adds a small amount of water if the heap gets dry.

....

....

.... **(2 marks)**

2 (a) It used to be common for food to be preserved by drying and/or salting. Explain how these help preserve food.

> Think about what causes food to decay and how drying and salting might prevent that happening.

Drying ....

....

Salting ....

....

.... **(3 marks)**

(b) More recent methods of preserving food include refrigeration and packing in nitrogen. Explain how these help preserve food.

Refrigeration ....

....

....

Packing in nitrogen ....

....

....

.... **(4 marks)**

Extended response – Ecosystems and material cycles

Explain how fish farming and other human activity have an impact on biodiversity.

> You will be more successful in extended response questions if you plan your answer before you start writing.
>
> Try to include a number of different examples of how human activity has an impact on biodiversity. Remember that not all human activity is bad for biodiversity; try to think of some examples where human activity can increase biodiversity.

....

....

....

....

....

....

....

....

....

....

....

....

....

....

....

....

....

....

....

....

....

....

.... **(6 marks)**

Timed Test 1

Time allowed: 1 hour 45 minutes

Total marks: 100

Edexcel publishes official Sample Assessment Material on its website. This practice exam paper has been written to help you practise what you have learned and may not be representative of a real exam paper.

1   Catalase is an enzyme found in many different tissues in plants and animals. It speeds up the breakdown of hydrogen peroxide:

hydrogen peroxide → water + oxygen

A group of students carried out an experiment to determine the amount of catalase in different plant and animal tissues. Their method is shown below.

> 1.   Add hydrogen peroxide solution to a test tube.
> 2.   Add a few drops of washing up liquid and shake gently to mix.
> 3.   Add a piece of plant or animal tissue.
> 4.   Measure the height of the foam produced by the oxygen after 30 seconds.

(a) Suggest a reason that explains why the students added a few drops of washing up liquid.   **(1 mark)**

(b) The students decided to use a water bath to control the temperature. Which temperature would be most suitable to use in their experiment?

   ☐   **A**   0 °C   ☐   **C**   60 °C

   ☐   **B**   20 °C   ☐   **D**   100 °C   **(1 mark)**

(c) State **two** variables, other than time or temperature, that the students should control in their investigation.   **(2 marks)**

(d) The students discovered that raw liver caused foaming in their experiment, but cooked liver did not. Suggest an explanation for these observations.   **(2 marks)**

(e) Explain why catalase will break down hydrogen peroxide, but it will not break down starch.   **(2 marks)**

(Total for Question 1 = 8 marks)

2   A man has an infection of disease-causing bacteria. He has not been immunised against these bacteria. The graph shows how the number of these bacteria change after a doctor gives the man a 7-day course of antibiotics.

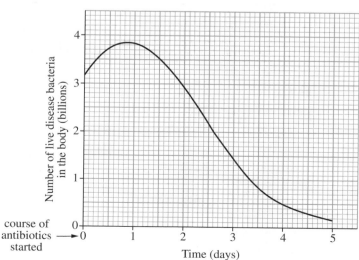

(a) Which of these is a typical feature of non-communicable diseases?

☐ **A** a pathogen is involved

☐ **B** cases are often localised

☐ **C** cases may be widely distributed

☐ **D** number of cases varies rapidly   **(1 mark)**

(b) Use the graph to determine:

(i) the time taken for the number of live bacteria to begin to fall after starting the course of antibiotics   **(1 mark)**

(ii) the maximum number of live disease bacteria in the man's body.   **(1 mark)**

(c) State whether the man has a communicable disease or a non-communicable disease. Give a reason for your answer.   **(1 mark)**

(d) The doctor suspected that the illness was caused by a bacterium rather than by a virus. Give **two** reasons that explain why the doctor was correct.   **(2 marks)**

(e) The man was told to take the antibiotic for the full seven days, even if he began to feel better.

(i) Explain why antibiotics can be used to treat bacterial infections.   **(2 marks)**

(ii) Give **two** reasons why it was important that the man did not stop taking the antibiotics early.   **(2 marks)**

(Total for Question 2 = 10 marks)

3 Gregor Mendel studied inheritance in peas and developed his three laws of inheritance. What Mendel called inherited 'factors' we now call genes.

(a) (i) Which of the following correctly describes a gene?

☐ **A** a pair of bases in DNA

☐ **B** a small section of protein that codes for a particular characteristic

☐ **C** a small section of DNA that codes for a particular characteristic

☐ **D** the characteristics that appear in an organism   **(1 mark)**

(ii) Draw a line to link each of the following terms to its corresponding definition.

homozygous		all the alleles in an organism
dominant		different forms of the same gene
allele		both alleles for one gene are the same
genotype		characteristic is seen only if both alleles are present
		characteristic is seen even if only one allele is present

(4 marks)

(b) One characteristic that Mendel studied was pod colour in peas. He crossed a pure-breeding plant with green pods with a pure-breeding plant with yellow pods.

  (i) Explain why Mendel used pure-breeding plants in his experiments.   **(2 marks)**

  (ii) All of the plants in the first generation of this cross had green pods.
       Suggest the conclusion Mendel made about the factor for green pods.   **(2 marks)**

(c) We now know that genes are represented by the order of bases in part of a molecule of DNA. DNA can be extracted from peas by the following method.

Crush peas with → Filter the → Add protease → Add ice-cold → Remove DNA
buffer solution   mixture   solution   ethanol
containing detergent

  (i) What is the function of the detergent?

  ☐ **A** break down the enzymes

  ☐ **B** supercoil the DNA

  ☐ **C** precipitate the DNA

  ☐ **D** disrupt cell membranes   **(1 mark)**

  (ii) State which substance is used to precipitate the DNA.   **(1 mark)**

  (Total for Question 3 = 11 marks)

4 The diagram shows a bacterial cell and a plant cell.

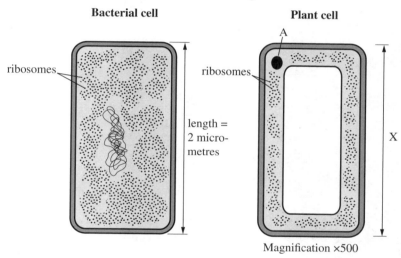

(a) State the name of structure A.   **(1 mark)**

(b) (i) Both types of cell contain ribosomes. State the function of a ribosome.   **(1 mark)**

  (ii) The plant cell contains mitochondria but the bacterial cell does not. State **two** other ways in which the plant cell is different to the bacterial cell.   **(2 marks)**

(c) Although the cells are drawn the same size, the magnifications are different. The actual length of the bacterial cell is 2 micrometres. Calculate the actual length, X, of the plant cell. Give your answer in micrometres. Show your working.   **(3 marks)**

(d) State, with an explanation, the type of microscope that would be used to examine each type of cell.   **(2 marks)**

  (Total for Question 4 = 9 marks)

5 The diagram shows a percentile chart developed by the US Government to monitor the growth of males between the ages of 2 and 20 years. It can be used to monitor both weight and height.

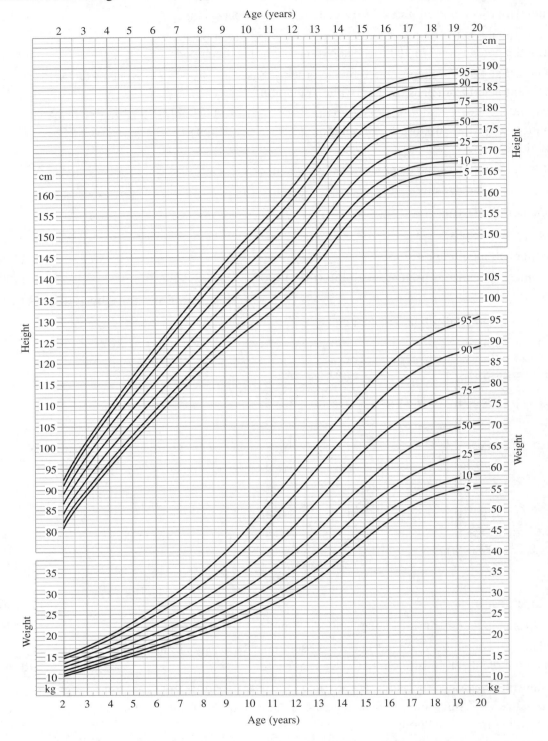

(a) Describe how a doctor or nurse could use this chart to monitor the growth of a boy from the age of 2 to 16 years. **(3 marks)**

(b) The table shows the weight and height records of two boys, A and B, from the ages of 4 to 16.

Age (years)	Height (cm)		Weight (kg)	
	Boy A	Boy B	Boy A	Boy B
4	102	105	18	17
8	127	132	32	27
12	148	155	56	42
16	170	179	83	60

(i) Plot the height and weight of Boy B on the chart above. Use 'o' for the points. The height and weight for Boy A have already been plotted using '+'. **(2 marks)**

(ii) Explain what your plotted points show about the development of the two boys. **(4 marks)**

(Total for Question 5 = 9 marks)

6 (a) Two proteins, DAZL and PRDM14, are involved in development of sperm cells. Mutations in these genes can increase the risk of developing testicular cancer. Almost 100% of all testicular cancers can be completely cured if diagnosed early.

Explain how the Human Genome Project has made it possible to improve treatment of men with a family history of testicular cancer. **(2 marks)**

(b) The human papilloma virus (HPV) is a sexually transmitted infection (STI). HPV infection causes genital warts but it can also lead to cervical cancer. HPV replicates by the lytic pathway and the lysogenic pathway.

(i) Describe **two** ways in which the lysogenic pathway is different from the lytic pathway. **(2 marks)**

(ii) Suggest why it can be a long time between being infected with HPV and the appearance of genital warts. **(2 marks)**

(c) 12- to 13-year-old girls are now being offered immunisation against HPV. Discuss the advantages and disadvantages of immunisation against HPV compared with other methods of preventing HPV infection. **(6 marks)**

(Total for Question 6 = 12 marks)

7 The diagram shows the neurones and other parts of the body involved in the response to touching a sharp object.

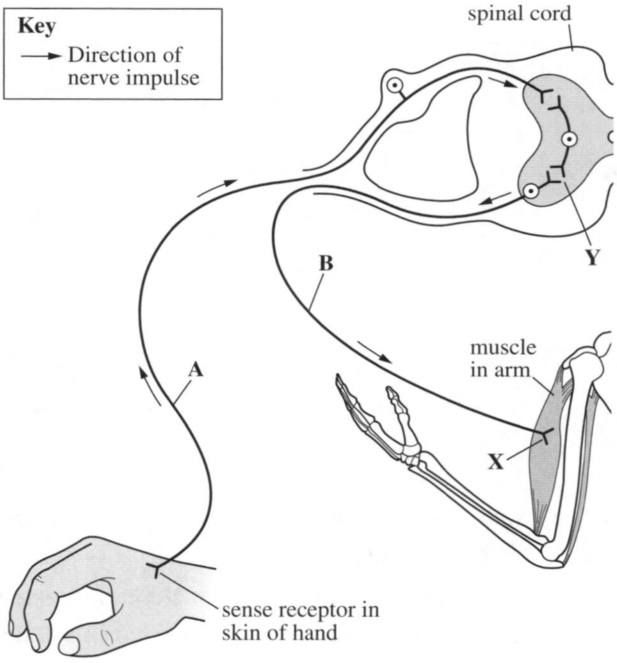

(a) Identify which of the following describes the correct sequence of events following touching a sharp object.

☐ **A** sensory receptor → sensory neurone → motor neurone → relay neurone

☐ **B** sensory receptor → muscle → motor neurone → relay neurone

☐ **C** sensory receptor → relay neurone → sensory neurone → motor neurone

☐ **D** sensory receptor → sensory neurone → relay neurone → motor neurone

(1 mark)

Key
→ Direction of nerve impulse

spinal cord

B

Y

muscle in arm

A

X

sense receptor in skin of hand

(b) (i) State the name of the structure labelled Y on the diagram. **(1 mark)**

(ii) Describe the events that occur at point Y that allow the impulse to be passed on from one neurone to the next. **(3 marks)**

(c) (i) Explain what would be the effect of an injury to the neurone labelled A. **(2 marks)**

(ii) Explain how the effect of damage to the spine in a road traffic accident would differ from injury to neurone A. **(3 marks)**

(Total for Question 7 = 10 marks)

8 A student was investigating the effect of two different antibiotics on the growth of bacteria. She prepared 10 agar plates containing either antibiotic A or antibiotic B. She then spread bacteria on each plate and incubated them for 3 days. After 3 days she counted the number of bacterial colonies on each plate. Her results are shown in the table.

	Number of bacterial colonies per plate					
	1	**2**	**3**	**4**	**5**	**Mean**
Antibiotic A	5	0	1	3	2	
Antibiotic B	55	50	54	53	56	

(a) (i)   State **one** precaution she should take to prevent growth of pathogenic bacteria.   **(1 mark)**

   (ii)   State **two** precautions she should take to prevent contamination of the plate with other microorganisms.   **(2 marks)**

(b) (i)   Calculate the mean number of colonies for antibiotic A, and for antibiotic B. Write your answers in the table.   **(2 marks)**

   (ii)   Describe what the results of the experiment show.   **(2 marks)**

(Total for Question 8 = 7 marks)

9 The graph shows the results of two studies into the effect of alcohol consumption on the risk of developing liver disease. One group (solid line) consisted only of males and the other group (dotted line) consisted only of females.

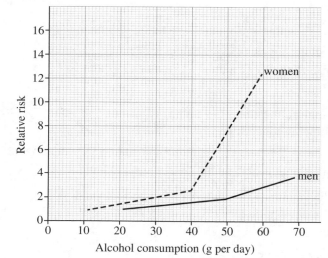

(a) State and explain the relationship between alcohol consumption and relative risk of liver disease for men.   **(3 marks)**

(b) The scientists concluded that alcohol intake was a greater risk for women than for men. Explain how their results supported this conclusion.   **(2 marks)**

(c) A patient has a height of 1.8 m and a body mass of 100 kg.

   What is his BMI?   **(1 mark)**

   ☐ **A** 30.9

   ☐ **B** 61.7

   ☐ **C** 27.8

   ☐ **D** 55.6

(Total for Question 9 = 6 marks)

10 (a) In humans there are two types of cell division: mitosis and meiosis. The table gives several statements about cell division. Tick one box in each row if the statement is true for mitosis only, for meiosis only or for both mitosis and meiosis. The first row has been completed for you.

Statement	Mitosis only	Meiosis only	Both mitosis and meiosis
used for growth and replacement of cells	✓		
used for production of gametes			
before the parent cell divides each chromosome is copied			
produces genetically identical cells			
halves the chromosome number			

(4 marks)

(b) There are two types of reproduction: sexual and asexual.

    (i) State **one** advantage and **one** disadvantage for sexual reproduction. **(2 marks)**

    (ii) State **one** advantage and **one** disadvantage for asexual reproduction. **(2 marks)**

(Total for Question 10 = 8 marks)

11 (a) What is a zygote?

    ☐   **A**   a male sex cell from a plant

    ☐   **B**   a female sex cell from an animal

    ☐   **C**   a haploid organism

    ☐   **D**   a cell formed at fertilisation   **(1 mark)**

(b) Complete the Punnett square to show how sex is inherited in humans.

		Parent 1 gametes	
		X	Y
Parent 2 gametes	X		
	X		

(1 mark)

(c) Use your answer to part (b) when answering these questions.

    (i) Which parent (1 or 2) is the father? Give a reason that explains your answer. **(1 mark)**

    (ii) State the probability of producing female offspring. **(1 mark)**

(Total for Question 11 = 4 marks)

12 Selective breeding is important in agriculture for the development of new strains of animals and plants. Describe how this is carried out. In your answer, include suitable examples. **(6 marks)**

(Total for Question 12 = 6 marks)

Timed Test 2

Time allowed: 1 hour 45 minutes

Total marks: 100

Edexcel publishes official Sample Assessment Material on its website. This practice exam paper has been written to help you practise what you have learned and may not be representative of a real exam paper.

1 (a) The diagram shows the apparatus used to measure the energy content of a piece of food. Once the food was burning, it was moved under the test tube and the temperature rise in the water was measured.

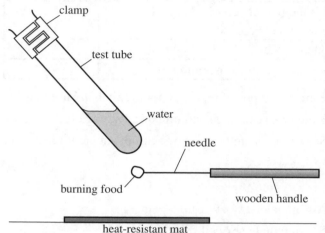

(i) Name **one** necessary piece of apparatus missing from the diagram.   **(1 mark)**

(ii) Give **two** reasons why the observed temperature rise might be less than expected.   **(2 marks)**

(iii) A bomb calorimeter is a device that gives an accurate measurement of the energy content of foods. In one experiment, 8.3 g of rice flour is completely burnt in a bomb calorimeter. The temperature of 500 g of water increases by 60.8 °C.
Use the equation below to calculate the energy transferred to heat the water:
energy transferred (J) = mass of water (g) × 4.2 × change in temperature (°C)
Calculate the energy content of rice flour in kJ/g.   **(3 marks)**

(b) Rice is the main food source for many people. The rice flour tested contained 80% carbohydrate and 6% protein.

(i) State the name of the test used to show that a food contains protein.   **(1 mark)**

(ii) State the colour you would see with a positive test for protein.   **(1 mark)**

(c) Scientists are developing new strains of rice with increased protein content.
Suggest an explanation for why this is important.   **(2 marks)**

(Total for Question 1 = 10 marks)

2 The graph shows the heart rate of an adult male over a 24-hour period.

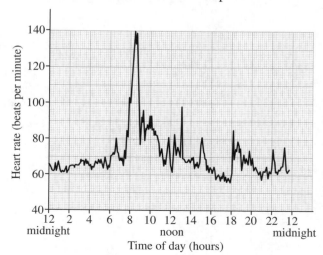

(a) (i)   Use the graph to estimate this person's resting heart rate.   **(1 mark)**

   (ii)   The man attended a 1-hour spinning (indoor cycling) class during the day.

      Use the graph to estimate the start time of the class.   **(1 mark)**

   (iii)   About an hour before the class started, the man walked uphill to the gym where the class was held. He then rested until the class started.

      Explain how the trace supports this.   **(2 marks)**

   (iv)   During the second half of the class, the man found it harder to maintain the cycling pace.

      Explain why the man found it harder to maintain the cycling pace.   **(2 marks)**

   (v)   The man noticed that his heart rate remained higher than normal for some time after the end of the class.

      Explain why his heart rate remained high after the class had finished.   **(2 marks)**

(b) (i)   The table shows the stroke volume and heart rate for two people measured while they were at rest. Complete the table by calculating the cardiac output for each person. Include the units for cardiac output.

	Stroke volume (cm^3)	Heart rate (beats per minute)	Cardiac output	Units
Person A	95	52		
Person B	58	72		

      (3 marks)

   (ii)   One person was a trained athlete, the other was untrained.

      Explain which was the trained athlete.   **(2 marks)**

                             (Total for Question 2 = 13 marks)

3   The diagram shows the part of the lung where gas exchange takes place.

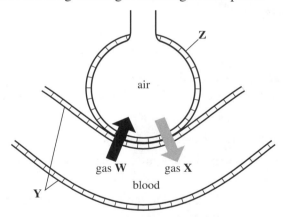

(a) (i)   State the names of the structures labelled **Y** and **Z** in the diagram.   **(2 marks)**

   (ii)   State which process is used to transport gases **W** and **X** in the directions shown.   **(1 mark)**

   (iii)   Give the name of gas **W**.   **(1 mark)**

   (iv)   Describe how gas **X** is carried in the blood.   **(1 mark)**

(b)   A scientist recently estimated that the average human lung has 480 million alveoli, and that 1 million alveoli have a surface area of 0.15 m^2.

   Calculate the total surface area of one human lung.   **(1 mark)**

(c)   Fick's law relates different factors to the rate of diffusion across a membrane.

   (i)   What changes will increase the rate of diffusion across a membrane?

		Concentration difference	Thickness of membrane
☐	A	decreased	decreased
☐	B	decreased	increased
☐	C	increased	increased
☐	D	increased	decreased

      (1 mark)

(ii) The surface area of the lungs may increase when an athlete trains regularly. Give a reason that explains why this may improve the athlete's performance. **(2 marks)**

(Total for Question 3 = 9 marks)

4 (a) The table lists several hormones, their site of production and target organ(s).

Choose from the following list of words to complete the table.

adrenalin	glucagon	kidney	muscle	oestrogen	ovaries
pancreas	pituitary gland	progesterone	testis	thyroid gland	

Hormone	Produced in	Target organ
ADH		
	adrenal gland	various organs, e.g. heart, liver, skin
glucagon		
	ovaries	pituitary gland

(4 marks)

(b) (i) Describe what happens in the uterus if an egg is not fertilised. **(2 marks)**

(ii) Explain how a hormone contraceptive pill prevents pregnancy. **(2 marks)**

(iii) Give **one** advantage of barrier methods of contraception compared with hormonal contraception. **(1 mark)**

(Total for Question 4 = 9 marks)

5 The survival of some organisms is dependent on other species. For example, the flea is an animal that feeds on the blood of other animals, including humans.

(a) Which term correctly describes a flea?

☐ **A** mutualist

☐ **B** parasite

☐ **C** producer

☐ **D** primary consumer **(1 mark)**

(b) An epiphyte is a type of plant that grows harmlessly on another species of plant. The epiphyte obtains its water and nutrients from air, rain and debris that accumulates around it.

(i) The mistletoe is a parasitic plant. Describe how a parasite differs from an epiphyte. **(2 marks)**

(ii) Describe **one** adaptation an epiphyte growing in a tropical rainforest might have. **(1 mark)**

(iii) Some epiphytes grow in places where there is little water. Describe **two** adaptations these plants might have to help them survive in these conditions. **(2 marks)**

(c) Nitrogen-fixing bacteria grow in nodules attached to the roots of some plants. The bacteria make nitrogen compounds that can be absorbed by the plant.

(i) Suggest **one** way in which the relationship benefits the bacteria. **(1 mark)**

(ii) Describe why the relationship between the bacteria and plants is described as mutualism. **(2 marks)**

(Total for Question 5 = 9 marks)

6 (a) The diagram is a light micrograph of a section of mouse tissue (magnification = 160×). The lighter shaded area is known as an islet and contains the cells responsible for producing insulin.

(i) The eyepiece on the microscope used was marked ×8.

Calculate the magnification of the objective lens used. **(2 marks)**

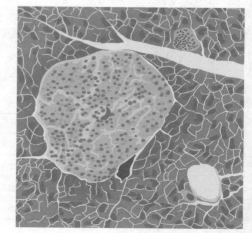

   (ii) Which of the following statements is correct?

   ☐   **A**   Insulin is made in the liver and acts on the kidney.

   ☐   **B**   Insulin is made in the liver and acts on the pancreas.

   ☐   **C**   Insulin is made in the pancreas and acts on the liver.

   ☐   **D**   Insulin is made in the muscles and acts on the liver.   **(1 mark)**

(b) (i) Explain why a person with Type 1 diabetes must inject themselves with insulin.   **(2 marks)**

   (ii) State **two** factors linked to development of Type 2 diabetes.   **(2 marks)**

(c) Homeostasis is the term used to describe how the internal environment of the body is kept constant and involves the process of negative feedback. Thermoregulation describes how the temperature of the body is maintained within a narrow range.

   Explain how thermoregulation operates to control body temperature.   **(6 marks)**

                                   (Total for Question 6 = 13 marks)

7 A group of students were undertaking a survey of an area of land alongside a path that crossed a field and entered a piece of woodland.

(a) (i) State **two** abiotic factors that might influence the distribution of plant species in the woodland.   **(2 marks)**

   (ii) State **two** biotic factors that might influence the distribution of plant species next to the path in the field.   **(2 marks)**

(b) Describe how the students should survey the abundance of different plant species growing alongside the path from the field and into the wood.   **(4 marks)**

                                   (Total for Question 7 = 8 marks)

8 A student carried out an investigation into osmosis in potato pieces. The student cut five pieces of potato, weighed them and then placed them into different concentrations of sucrose solution. After one hour the student removed the potato pieces from the sucrose solution and weighed them again. The student's results are shown in the table.

Concentration of sucrose solution (mol dm^{-3})	Initial mass of potato (g)	Final mass of potato (g)	Percentage change in mass (%)
0.0	5.2	5.4	
0.5	5.6	5.6	
1.0	5.6	5.4	−3.6
2.0	5.0	4.6	−8.0
3.0	5.2	4.2	−19.2

(a) (i) Complete the table by calculating the percentage change in mass of the potato pieces. Give your answers to one decimal place.   **(3 marks)**

   (ii) State **one** variable the student would need to control during the experiment.   **(1 mark)**

   (iii) Describe **one** way in which the student could improve the experiment.   **(1 mark)**

   (iv) Use the results to estimate the solute concentration of the potato cells.

       Explain your answer.   **(2 marks)**

(b) People with kidney failure can be treated with dialysis.

   Describe how dialysis works to make sure that the patient's blood has the right concentration of substances.   **(4 marks)**

                                     (Total for Question 8 = 11 marks)

9 (a) The diagram shows a specialised type of plant tissue.

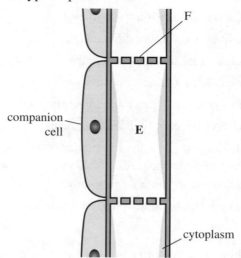

companion cell

E

F

cytoplasm

(i) Which specialised plant tissue is shown in the diagram?

☐ **A** xylem   ☐ **C** mesophyll

☐ **B** phloem   ☐ **D** root hair   **(1 mark)**

(ii) Identify the parts labelled E and F.   **(2 marks)**

(b) The companion cells contain large numbers of mitochondria.

(i) What is the function of a mitochondrion?

☐ **A** to carry out photosynthesis

☐ **B** to carry out respiration

☐ **C** to control the entry of substances to the cell

☐ **D** to control the activities of the cell   **(1 mark)**

(ii) Suggest an explanation for why the companion cell contains large numbers of mitochondria.   **(2 marks)**

(c) (i) Temperature can be a limiting factor in photosynthesis. State **one** other factor that can limit the rate of photosynthesis.   **(1 mark)**

(ii) The graph shows how the rate of photosynthesis changes as temperature is increased.

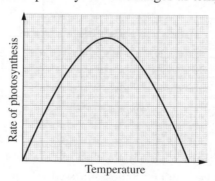

Rate of photosynthesis

Temperature

Explain why the rate of photosynthesis changes as the temperature is increased.   **(3 marks)**

(Total for Question 9 = 10 marks)

10 (a) Which of the following statements about food security is true?

☐ **A** Fish farming reduces reliance on wild fish.

☐ **B** Improved agriculture methods reduce food security.

☐ **C** Much more protein can be produced from meat animals than from growing soybean on the same area of land.

☐ **D** Growing crops to produce biofuels increases food security.   **(1 mark)**

(b) Sea lice infest wild and farmed salmon. The graph shows the mean number of sea lice per salmon in farmed salmon in Ireland. New control measures were introduced in 2007.

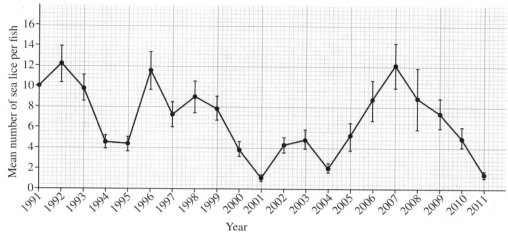

Calculate the percentage increase in the mean number of sea lice per salmon between 2004 and 2007.

                                                    (1 mark)

(c) Killary Harbour is a 16-kilometre fjord on the west coast of Ireland where two types of aquaculture are carried out – salmon farming and mussel farming. Mussel farming involves suspending ropes in the water and mussel 'seed' (immature shellfish) are attached. The mussels then grow naturally over a period of 12–15 months. Mussels feed on microscopic organisms that they filter from the sea water. This can remove phosphates and nitrates from the water. Some people are opposed to salmon farming because they believe it is harmful to the environment. In contrast with salmon farming, mussel farming is thought to have less impact on the environment.

Evaluate the two types of aquaculture in terms of their environmental impact.   **(6 marks)**

(Total for Question 10 = 8 marks)

Answers

1. Plant and animal cells

1 (a) B **(1)**

   (b) C **(1)**

2 (a) carry out respiration **(1)**, releasing energy for cell processes **(1)**

   (b) Mitochondria release energy and all cells need energy **(1)**, but only leaf (and stem) cells are exposed to light and so have chloroplasts for photosynthesis **(1)**.

3 Cell membrane controls what enters and leaves the cell **(1)**; cell wall helps to support the cell / helps it keep its shape **(1)**.

4 Ribosomes are where proteins are made **(1)**; pancreatic cells produce large amounts of proteins but fat cells do not **(1)**.

2. Different kinds of cell

1 C **(1)**

2 (a) A = acrosome **(1)**; B = flagellum **(1)**

   (b) A contains enzymes to digest a way through the egg cell membrane **(1)**; B is used to move the bacterium towards a food source **(1)**.

3 Epithelial cells line tubes (such as trachea) **(1)**. Mucus traps dirt / dust / bacteria **(1)** and cilia move mucus along the tubes away from the lungs **(1)**.

3. Microscopes and magnification

1 Light microscopes magnify less than electron microscopes **(1)**. The level of cell detail seen with an electron microscope is greater **(1)**, because electron microscopes have a higher resolution **(1)**.

2 (a) because it has a nucleus **(1)** and eukaryotic cells have nuclei **(1)**

   (b) (i) $(23 / 5) \times 2$ **(1)** = 9.2 μm **(1)**

      (ii) $(4 / 5) \times 2$ **(1)** = 1.6 μm **(1)**

   (c) Nuclei are large enough to be seen with a light microscope **(1)** but mitochondria are too small and can be seen only with an electron microscope **(1)** because it has a higher resolution / greater magnification **(1)**.

3 (a) light microscope: 2.5 μm × 1000 **(1)** = 2500 μm (or 2.5 mm) **(1)**; electron microscope: 2.5 μm × 100 000 = 250 000 μm (or 250 mm or 25 cm or 0.25 m) **(1)** (Note that you get the mark for correct use of the formula just once even though you use it twice.)

   (b) The electron microscope **(1)** because it would show more detail / has the correct resolution **(1)**

4. Dealing with numbers

1 picometre, nanometre, micrometre, millimetre, metre **(1)**

2 5 picometres **(1)**, 0.25 grams **(1)**, 0.00025 kilograms **(1)**, 2500 millimetres **(1)**

3 true **(1)**, false **(1)**, false **(1)**, true **(1)**

4 (a) 30.9 / 1 000 000 = 0.0000309 mm **(1)** = 30.9 nm **(1)**

   (b) 163 / 250 000 = 0.000652 mm **(1)** = 652 nm **(1)**

   (c) 7.8 / 800 = 0.0975 mm **(1)** = 9.8 μm **(1)**

5. Using a light microscope

1 (a) (i) to reflect light through the slide **(1)**

      (ii) to hold the slide in place **(1)**

      (iii) to move the objective up and down a long way **(1)**

   (b) (i) because it could crash into the slide **(1)**

      (ii) because it could permanently damage eyesight **(1)**

   (c) (i) a desk / bench / built-in lamp **(1)**

      (ii) Two from: always start with the lowest power objective under the eyepiece **(1)**; clip the slide securely on the stage **(1)**; move the slide so the cell you need is in the middle of the (low-power) view **(1)**; use only the fine focusing wheel with the high-power objective **(1)**

2 Three from: go back to using the low-power objective **(1)**; find the part you need and bring it back to the centre view **(1)**; focus on it with the coarse focus **(1)**; return to the high-power objective **(1)** and use the fine focus wheel to bring the part into focus **(1)**.

6. Drawing labelled diagrams

1 (a) Three from: the drawing is in pen rather than pencil **(1)**; the title is incomplete **(1)**; the magnification is not given **(1)**; label lines are not drawn with a ruler **(1)** and cross each other **(1)**; not enough cells are shown **(1)** and they are not drawn to scale **(1)**; shading should not be used **(1)**; lines have been crossed out rather than rubbed out **(1)** and are ragged rather than clear **(1)**; the cell membrane can't be seen with the light microscope **(1)**

   (b) Clear drawing of all / most of the cells **(1)**; cells not of interest drawn just as outlines **(1)**; detail of representative sample of cells **(1)**; and avoidance of mistakes from 1 (a) **(1)**

2 Width of image = 45 mm **(1)** so magnification = 45 / 0.113 **(1)** = ×398 (or 400) **(1)**

7. Enzymes

1 The shape of the active site of invertase matches the shape of sucrose but not lactose **(1)**, so invertase cannot combine with lactose and catalyse its digestion **(1)**.

2 (a) Answer in the range 43–45 °C **(1)**

   (b) D **(1)**

   (c) As the temperature increases, the rate of collisions increases **(1)** between the substrate and active site **(1)**.

3 Optimum pH of pepsin is about 2 **(1)**; optimum pH of trypsin is about 8 **(1)**; these are the same as the pH in the stomach and small intestine **(1)**.

8. pH and enzyme activity

1 (a)

pH	2	4	6	8	10
Time (min)	> 10	7.5	3.6	1.2	8.3
Rate (min)	0	0.13	**0.28**	**0.83**	**0.12**

   (**2 marks** for all 5 correct, **1 mark** for 3 correct)

   (b)

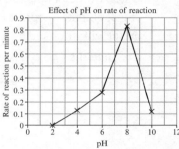

Effect of pH on rate of reaction

   correctly plotted points **(1)**, points joined by straight lines / line of best fit (can be smooth curve) **(1)**

   (c) Two from: use a water bath to control temperature **(1)**; repeat several times and take a mean **(1)**; use a more accurate method to determine if the film is clear **(1)**; use more intermediate pH values **(1)**

9. The importance of enzymes

1

Enzyme	Digests	Product(s)
amylase	starch	**sugars / maltose**
lipase	**lipids**	**fatty acids and glycerol**
protease	**proteins**	amino acids

   1 mark for each correct row.

2 (a) Many different enzymes are needed because they are specific for different food molecules **(1)**; digestion breaks down the food molecules into molecules small enough to be absorbed **(1)**.

   (b) Synthesis reactions occur too slowly **(1)**; enzymes are biological catalysts and speed up reactions **(1)**.

3 (a) lipase *and* protease boxes ticked only **(1)**

(b) The enzyme is denatured / active site destroyed (1) at higher temperatures (1), so it would not digest stains as well / would be less active (1).

4 Both involve enzymes (1); digestion involves breaking down large molecules to form small molecules (1) but synthesis involves producing large molecules from smaller molecules (1).

10. Using reagents in food tests

1 (a) (i) wear eye protection / lab coat / gloves (1)

   (ii) iodine can stain the skin / clothing (1)

   (b) Mix the food with ethanol and shake (1); pour some of the mixture into water and shake again (1); cloudy emulsion will form if lipids present (1).

2 (a) C (1)

   (b) Heat water in a kettle (1); pour hot water into a beaker and place the test tubes in the water (1).

3 (a) The broad bean contained protein. (1)

   (b) Add iodine solution (1); turns black/blue-black if starch is present (1).

11. Using calorimetry

1 (a) the final/maximum temperature of the water (1)

   (b) Two from: starting temperature of the water (1); temperature increase (1); temperature of the room (1); heating time (1); distance of flame/snack from the bottom of the boiling tube (1); mass of snack (1)

   (c) (i) Snack A: 2940 J (1); Snack B: 20 × 4.2 × 27 = 2268 J (1)

   (ii) Snack A: 2940/2.5 = 1175 J/g (1); 1200 J/g to 2 sig. fig. (1); Snack B: 2268/2.0 = 1134 J/g (1); 1100 J/g to 2 sig. fig. (1)

   (d) One from: the snack may not have been completely burned (1); not all the energy was transferred to the water (1); some energy was transferred to the surroundings (1); the sample of food was very small / not representative of the snack (1)

12. Getting in and out of cells

1 Movement of particles (1) from high concentration to low concentration / down a concentration gradient (1).

2 One mark for each correct row to 4 marks:

Feature	Diffusion	Active transport
Involves the movement of particles	✓	✓
Requires energy		✓
Can happen across a partially permeable membrane	✓	✓
Net movement down a concentration gradient	✓	

3 (a) Osmosis is the net movement of water molecules (1) across a partially permeable membrane (1) from a low solute concentration (1) to a high solute concentration (1).

   (b) Diffusion (1); because movement is from a high concentration to a low concentration / down a concentration gradient (1)

   (c) Glucose must be moved against a concentration gradient (1) by active transport that requires energy (1).

13. Osmosis in potatoes

1 Four from: Cut pieces of potato, making sure size / length is the same (1); measure mass (1); leave in solution for 20 minutes / same time (1). Remove from the solution, then measure mass again (1). Blot dry before each weighing (1).

2 (a) missing change in mass: 0.25 (1); missing percentage change = (−0.15/2.58) × 100 = −5.8 % (1)

   (b) points plotted ± half square (1); line of best fit (1)

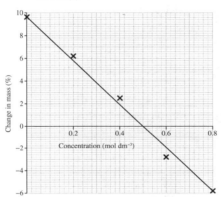

   (c) answer in the range 0.45 mol dm⁻³ to 0.55 mol dm⁻³ (1)

14. Extended response – Key concepts

*Answer could include the following points to 6 marks:
Similarities: both have:
- cell membrane, which controls what enters and leaves the cell
- cell wall, which strengthens the cell
- cytoplasm, in which cell reactions happen
- ribosomes, where protein synthesis happens.
Differences:
- plant cells have mitochondria, where respiration happens, but bacterial cells do not
- plant cells have chloroplasts, where photosynthesis happens, but bacterial cells do not
- DNA, which contains genetic information, is contained in a nucleus in plant cells, but is found in a single chromosome / loop and in plasmids in bacterial cells
- cell wall in plant cells is made from cellulose but from different substances in bacterial cells
- plant cells have a permanent vacuole filled with cell sap, which helps to keep the cell rigid, but bacterial cells do not.

15. Mitosis

1 (a) B (1)

   (b) interphase, prophase, metaphase, anaphase, telophase (1)

2 To produce new individuals by asexual reproduction (1); for growth (1); for repair (1)

3 (a) A = anaphase (1); B = metaphase (1)

   (b) A is because chromatids are being pulled to each pole (1); B is because chromosomes are lined up along the middle of the cell (1).

16. Cell growth and differentiation

1 (a) zygote (1)

   (b) mitosis (1)

2 (a) meristem / root tip / shoot tip (1)

   (b) Vacuoles take in water by osmosis (1) and this causes the cell to elongate (1).

3 (a)

Type of specialised cell	Animal or plant
sperm	animal
xylem	**plant**
ciliated cell	**animal**
root hair cell	**plant**
egg cell	**animal**

   3 marks for 4 or 5 correct, **2 marks** for 3 correct, **1 mark** for 2 correct.

   (b) Plants: mesophyll cell / guard cell / phloem (1). Animals: small intestine cell / hepatocyte / red blood cell / nerve cell / bone cell / (smooth) muscle cell (1).

4 (a) Cells become specialised (1) to perform a particular function (1).

   (b) Many different kinds of specialised cells (1) can carry out different processes more effectively (1).

17. Growth and percentile charts

1 (a) C (1)

   (b) 47.5 − 46.0 (1) = 1.5 cm (± 0.2 cm) (1)

2 (a) 15.35 − 12.75 = 2.60 g (1); (2.60 / 12.75) × 100 = 20.4% (1)

   (b) Any suitable, such as: height (1), measured with a ruler ensuring the stem is vertical (1); shoots / leaves (1) by counting number (1)

18. Stem cells

1 (a) A (1)

   (b) (i) meristem (1)

   (ii) tips of root (1) and tips of shoot (1)

2 (a) to replace damaged / worn-out cells (1)

   (b) Differentiated cells cannot divide / embryonic stem cells can divide, to produce other kinds of cell (1).

3 (a) Embryonic stem cells could be stimulated to produce nerve cells (1) then transplanted into the patient's brain (1).

   (b) (i) does not destroy embryos / patient's immune system will not reject them (1)

   (ii) may cause cancer / may not differentiate into nerve cells (1)

19. The brain and spinal cord

1 (a) brain **and** spinal cord (1)

   (b) (i) regulates heartbeat / breathing (1)

Answers

(ii) coordinates and controls precise and smooth movement (**1**)

(c) Two from: control voluntary movement (**1**); interpret sensory information (**1**); responsible for learning (**1**) and memory (**1**)

2 medulla oblongata (**1**), cerebral hemispheres (**1**), cerebellum **and** cerebral hemispheres (**1**), cerebral hemispheres (**1**)

3 Her running is coordinated by the cerebellum, which controls smooth movement and keeps her balanced (**1**). The cerebral hemispheres (**1**) interpret the sensory information from her ears while listening to music and also from her eyes when she sees her friend. Her heart rate and breathing rate are controlled by the medulla oblongata (**1**). Waving to her friend is controlled by the cerebral hemispheres (**1**).

4 He would become paralysed (**1**); permanently / from the site of the cut downwards (**1**); neurones cannot divide to replace/repair damaged neurones (**1**); nerve impulses would not be able to travel to parts of the body below the damage (**1**).

20. Neurones

1 motor neurone – carries impulses from the central nervous system to effectors (**1**); relay neurone – carries impulses from one part of the central nervous system to another (**1**); sensory neurone – carries impulses to the central nervous system (**1**)

2 A, axon endings; B, axon; C, cell body; D, dendron; E, myelin sheath; F, receptor cells (in skin) (all correct, **3 marks**; 4 or 5 correct, **2 marks**; 2 or 3 correct, **1 mark**)

3 The axon is long so it can carry impulses over long distances (**1**). The axon has a myelin sheath which is an electrical insulator / prevents impulses passing to neighbouring neurones (**1**). The nerve ending transmits impulses to effectors/glands/muscles (**1**).

4 (a) Myelin sheath speeds up transmission (**1**) because the impulse jumps from one gap to another (**1**).

(b) Their movement would be impaired / made difficult (**1**) because the nerve impulses to muscles would be slower / can move between adjacent neurones (**1**).

21. Responding to stimuli

1 In any order: innate (**1**); automatic (**1**); rapid (**1**)

2 (a) synapse (**1**)

(b) Neurone Y (**1**); because it is carrying impulses to an effector / muscle (**1**)

(c) When an electrical impulse reaches the end of neurone X it causes the release of neurotransmitter (**1**) into the gap between the neurones. This substance diffuses (**1**) across the synapse / gap (**1**) and causes neurone Y to generate an electrical impulse (**1**).

3 (a) Three from: Stimulus is detected by receptors (**1**); a nerve impulse travels along a sensory neurone (**1**) then through a relay neurone in the brain / CNS / spinal cord (**1**) and along a motor neurone to an effector (**1**).

(b) light / movement (**1**) because it causes the eyelid to blink (**1**)

22. The eye

1 (a) A cornea, B pupil, C lens, D iris, E ciliary muscles, F retina (**3 marks** for all correct, **2 marks** for 4 or 5 correct, **1 mark** for 2 or 3 correct)

(b) Both are transparent to let light through (**1**); both are curved to refract / bend / focus light (**1**); the shape of the lens can change / become more or less curved (**1**).

2 The iris changes its size by muscle contraction and relaxation (**1**). It does this to control how much light enters (**1**).

3 (a) To form an image the light rays must converge / be focused / be refracted (**1**) onto the retina (**1**). This occurs as light passes from air through the curved surface of the cornea and lens (**1**).

(b) (The ciliary muscles contract) making the lens fatter (**1**), so increasing the refraction / causing the light to bend or converge more (**1**).

4 They need to be able to see in very dim light (**1**) and rod cells are sensitive at low light intensity (**1**), whereas cones work only in bright light (**1**).

23. Eye problems

1 (a) short sight (**1**)

(b) The lens makes the light rays diverge (**1**), so that the image moves away from the lens / closer to the retina (**1**).

(c) (i) Must be clean / free of microbes to avoid infections. (**1**)

(ii) The cells in the cornea need oxygen for respiration / to stay alive. (**1**)

2 Vision is blurred (**1**) because light cannot pass through to the retina properly (**1**).

3 As they get older the lens does not bend enough (**1**) and so they cannot focus on close objects (**1**).

4 (a) cone(s) (**1**)

(b) Either red or green cones are missing (**1**) so the person cannot distinguish between red and green (**1**).

24. Extended response – Cells and control

*Answer could include the following points:

● Stages of mitosis described as part of the cell cycle.
● Production of genetically identical daughter cells.
● Diploid number maintained in all cells except gametes.
● Involves replication of DNA.
● Description of cell differentiation.
● Examples of specialised cell types.
● Importance of stem cells: in embryo to produce all different kinds of cell in the body; in adult for growth and repair.

25. Asexual and sexual reproduction

1

Feature	Sexual reproduction	Asexual reproduction
need to find a mate	needs to find a mate	no need to find a mate
mixing of genetic information	mixes genetic information from each parent	no mixing of genetic information
characteristics of offspring	offspring show variety of characteristics	offspring have same characteristics as parent / each other

1 mark for each correct row.

2 (a) runners: asexual (**1**) because only one parent / offspring all identical to parent (**1**); fruits: sexual (**1**) because there are two parents / fusion of gametes (**1**)

(b) asexual: plant can make use of beneficial conditions because more plants produced quickly (**1**); sexual: offspring may be better adapted if conditions change because of variation (**1**) OR prevents overcrowding because seeds spread more widely (**1**)

(c) asexual: no genetic variation so plants may die / not grow as well if conditions change (**1**); sexual: requires two parents (pollination) / requires energy to produce fruits (**1**)

3 Two from: energy needed to find a mate (**1**), in courtship behaviour (**1**), in gamete production (**1**)

26. Meiosis

1 (a) (i) half the number of chromosomes / one set of chromosomes (**1**)

(ii) sex cells (**1**)

(b) male: sperm (**1**); female: egg / ovum (**1**)

2 (a) 10 (**1**)

(b) Each daughter cell has only half of chromosomes / genes / DNA from each parent (**1**) so different daughter cells have different combinations of chromosomes / genes / DNA (**1**)

3 (a) DNA replication (**1**)

(b)

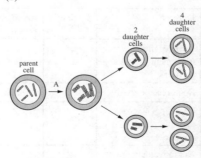

2 daughter cells, then 4 daughter cells (**1**), one of each pair consisting of duplicated chromosomes in 2 daughter cells (**1**); 4

daughter cells contain one copy of each pair **(1)**

4   Mitosis maintains the diploid number **(1)** and produces cells that are identical to the parent cell **(1)**. It is used for growth **(1)**. Meiosis creates gametes that have half the number of chromosomes **(1)**. Fertilisation restores the diploid number **(1)**.

27. DNA

1   (a) genome **(1)**

    (b) A chromosome consists of a long molecule of DNA packed with proteins **(1)**; a gene is a section of DNA molecule / section of chromosome that codes for a specific protein **(1)**. DNA is the molecule containing genetic information that forms part of the chromosomes **(1)**.

2   (a) double helix **(1)**

    (b) (i) 4 **(1)**

       (ii) weak hydrogen bonds between complementary bases **(1)**

3   (a) The structure consists of repeated nucleotides / monomers **(1)**.

    (b) A base **(1)**, B sugar / ribose **(1)**, C phosphate **(1)**

4   A **(1)**

28. Gregor Mendel

1   (a) Red hair is either present or absent **(1)** and a parent with red hair may not have red-haired children **(1)**.

    (b) These could not be caused by blending **(1)** because the characteristics were either present or absent **(1)**.

2   (a) so that he would know what factors they had **(1)** because they always produce identical offspring when crossed with a pea of the same type **(1)**

    (b) Experiment 1: the factor for yellow seeds was dominant to the factor for green seeds **(1)** because the first generation all produced yellow seeds **(1)**

    Experiment 2: the factor for round seeds was dominant to the factor for wrinkled seeds **(1)** because the first generation all produced round seeds **(1)**.

    (c) yellow round seeds **(1)**

29. Genetic terms

1   (a) (i) different forms of the same gene that produce different variations of the characteristic **(1)**

      (ii) Genotype shows the alleles that are present in the individual, e.g. Bb or BB **(1)**, whereas phenotype means the characteristics that are produced, e.g. brown eyes or blue eyes **(1)**.

    (b) bb **(1)**, BB **(1)**, Bb **(1)**

    (c) bb **(1)** because to have blue eyes she must have two recessive alleles **(1)**

2   There are two copies of each chromosome in body cells **(1)**; each copy has the same genes in the same order **(1)**; a gene is a short piece of DNA at a point on a chromosome **(1)**; genes come in different forms called alleles that produce different variations of the characteristic **(1)**.

30. Monohybrid inheritance

1   (a) correct gametes **(1)**; correct genotypes **(1)**

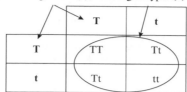

	T	t
T	TT	Tt
t	Tt	tt

    (b) 25% of the offspring from this cross will be short **(1)**. I know this because tt is short **(1)** and one in four of the possible offspring is tt. **(1)**

    (c) $\frac{3}{4}$ or 75% **(1)**

2   (a) Completed Punnett square:

		Parent genotype Gg	
	Parent gametes	G	g
Parent genotype gg	g	Gg	gg
	g	Gg	gg

    Parent gametes correct **(1)**; offspring genotypes correct **(1)**

    (b) 20 **(1)**

31. Family pedigrees

1   C **(1)**

2   (a) two **(1)**

    (b) one **(1)**

    (c) Person 4 does not have cystic fibrosis. This means that she must have one dominant allele from her father **(1)**. But she must have inherited a recessive allele from her mother **(1)**. This means that her genotype is Ff **(1)**.

    (d) Two healthy parents (person 3 & person 4) **(1)** produce a child (person 8) with CF **(1)**.

32. Sex determination

1   (a) X **(1)**; the girl has two X chromosomes, one from each parent **(1)**

    (b) (i) **1 mark** for parental sex chromosomes and **1 mark** for all possible children's chromosomes

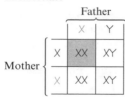

      (ii) female **(1)**

2   (a) 50% / ½ / 0.5 **(1)**; depends on which sperm fertilises the egg **(1)** as half the sperm will carry a male sex chromosome / Y chromosome and half the sperm will carry a female sex chromosome / X chromosome **(1)**

    (b) The statement is not correct **(1)**; the probability of having a child who is a boy is always 50% **(1)**.

33. Inherited characteristics

1   This is when a heterozygous individual shows the effect of both alleles **(1)**.

2   (a) A = $I^A I^A$ **(1)**; AB = $I^A I^B$ **(1)**

    (b) group AB, $I^A I^B$ **(1)**; because some children received the I^B allele from the mother **(1)** and others received the I^A allele **(1)**.

    (c) A child who is group B must receive an I^B allele from each parent **(1)**, but the man only has I^A alleles so cannot be the father **(1)**.

3   (a) Completed Punnett square:

		Parent genotype $I^A I^B$	
	Parent gametes	I^A	I^B
Parent genotype IAIB	I^A	$I^A I^A$ A	$I^A I^B$ AB
	I^B	$I^A I^B$ AB	$I^B I^B$ B

    Parent gametes correct **(1)**; offspring genotypes correct **(1)**; offspring blood groups correct **(1)**

    (b) A 25% / ¼; AB 50% / ½; B 25% / ¼

34. Variation and mutation

1   (a) Students in a year 7 class will show differences in mass caused by genetic variation **(1)** as well as environmental variation. **(1)** Can be opposite order.

    (b) Identical twins will show differences caused only by environmental variation **(1)**.

2   (a) mean height = (181 + 184 + 178 + 190 + 193 + 179) / 6 **(1)** = 184.2 cm **(1)**

    (b) Four from: height is determined partly by genetic factors **(1)** and partly by environmental factors **(1)** such as nutrition **(1)**; different children have inherited different alleles from their parents **(1)**; parents have different heights so will pass on different alleles for height **(1)**; the mean height of the children is greater than that of the parents because of better nutrition / they take after their father more than their mother **(1)**

3   (a) a change in an organism's DNA **(1)** such as a change in a gene / sequence of bases **(1)**

    (b) Two from: no effect **(1)**, small effect **(1)**, significant effect **(1)** on phenotype

35. The Human Genome Project

1   (a) the sequence of bases on all human chromosomes **(1)**

    (b) Advantages, two from: a person at risk from a genetic condition will be alerted **(1)**; distinguishing between different forms of disease **(1)**; tailoring treatments for some diseases to the individual **(1)**

    Disadvantages: people at risk of some diseases may have to pay more for life insurance **(1)**; it may not be helpful to tell someone they are at risk from an incurable disease **(1)**

2   Advantages, any two from: she could have earlier / more frequent screening for breast cancer **(1)**, she could consider surgery to remove the breast / mastectomy **(1)**, her doctor might prescribe drugs to reduce the risk of developing cancer **(1)**; disadvantages, any two from: it might make her more worried / anxious **(1)**, just because she has the mutation doesn't mean she will develop breast cancer **(1)**, could have unnecessary surgery / medication **(1)**

Answers

36. Extended response – Genetics

*Answer could include the following points:
- Factors are genes, versions of factors are alleles.
- Two sets of chromosomes carry the same genes, but may have different alleles of each gene.
- Meiosis means each gamete receives only one of each allele (factor).
- Alleles on different chromosomes will be inherited randomly.
- If both alleles are the same the organism is homozygous, if they are different it is heterozygous.
- Dominant alleles will always be expressed.
- Recessive alleles are only expressed in homozygous organisms.
- The more powerful factors are dominant alleles.
- The less powerful/weaker factors are recessive alleles.

37. Evolution

1 (a) Any two from: theory involved natural selection (**1**); theory was based on their own work / work of previous scientists (**1**); they presented their work jointly in 1858 (**1**)

   (b) All correct for **2 marks**, two correct for **1 mark**, deduct one mark if third row is ticked:

Possible impact	Correct (✓)
Helps us understand the relationships between different species	✓
Explains how new species evolve	✓
Explains how life on Earth first began	
Explains how different species adapt to changes in their environment	✓

2 There is variation within a species (**1**); members of the species that are most adapted will survive / those that are less well adapted die (**1**).

3 It will help to classify the new species (**1**) and to find out which other organisms the new species is related to (**1**).

4 There is variation in the amount of antibiotic resistance in a population of bacteria (**1**); the most resistant take the longest to die (**1**), so stopping early means the most resistant survive and reproduce (**1**) so that all the new population of bacteria will be resistant (**1**).

38. Human evolution

1 Three from: toe arrangement (**1**), length of arms (**1**), brain size (**1**), skull shape (**1**)

2 (a) Two from: the older the species, the smaller its brain volume (**1**); negative correlation / as years before present became less, brain volume increased OR positive correlation – as time 'increases' brain volume increases (**1**); greatest increase in brain volume between 2.4 and 1.8 million years ago (**1**); increase in brain volume not linear, but increased by 500 cm^3 in 2.6 million years (**1**)

   (b) an increase in brain volume / size (**1**) to at least 550 cm^3 (**1**)

3 (a) The ages of the rock layers where the tool was found can be dated (**1**) by measuring the amount of radiation in the layers (**1**).

   (b) Three from: smooth area in palm of hand (**1**), will not cut / damage hand (**1**); chipped section away from hand (**1**) (as it) has sharp edges (**1**) for cutting / unlike smooth area (**1**)

39. Classification

1 Both have limbs with five fingers (**1**) that have evolved / become adapted to different uses (**1**).

2 Plants are autotrophic feeders but animals are heterotrophic feeders (**1**). Plant cells have cells walls but animal cells do not (**1**). *Could also say* animal cells do not contain chlorophyll / plant cells contain chlorophyll (**1**)

3 Panther / *Panthera pardus* and wolf / *Canis lupus* (**1**); because they both belong to the same (kingdom, phylum, class and) order (**1**)

4 (a) C (**1**)

   (b) genetic research / research on genes (**1**)

40. Selective breeding

1 (a) Plants or animals with certain desirable characteristics are chosen to breed together (**1**) so that their offspring will inherit these characteristics (**1**).

   (b) Pigs with lower body fat are crossed (**1**); offspring with low body fat are selected and crossed (**1**); repeated for many generations until a lean breed is produced (**1**).

2 (a) high yield so can feed more people (**1**); low fertiliser requirement so no need to apply fertiliser / reduce cost (**1**); pest resistant (or example given) so less pest damage / do not need to apply pesticide (**1**)

   (b) drought resistant to cope with times of water shortage without dying (**1**); tolerant of high temperature (**1**)

3 Three from: alleles that might be useful in the future might no longer be available (**1**); a new disease might affect all organisms (**1**); selectively bred organisms might not adapt to changes in climate (**1**); animal welfare might be harmed (**1**)

41. Genetic engineering

1 (a) D (**1**)

   (b) (i) One from: resistance to herbicides (**1**); production of beta-carotene (**1**)

      (ii) One from: increased crop yields (**1**); less insecticide needed (**1**)

      (iii) One from: may kill insect species that are not pests (**1**); less food for birds (**1**); gene for insect resistance may transfer to another species of plant (**1**)

2 The gene from a jellyfish (**1**) is cut out using enzymes. (**1**) This gene is transferred to a mouse (**1**) embryo cell, and inserted into a chromosome. The embryo is then allowed to develop as normal.

3 Four from: GM bacteria produce human insulin not pig insulin (**1**); so this will be more effective/is the right form of insulin/is

less likely to cause adverse reactions (**1**); can be produced in large quantities by the bacteria (**1**); this means that it can be produced at low cost (**1**); some people would have ethical/ religious objections to having insulin from pigs (**1**)

42. Tissue culture

1 (a) genetically identical individuals (**1**)

   (b) to make useful plant products such as anticancer drugs and to (**1**) (one from): produce disease-free plants (**1**); help to preserve rare plant species (**1**); produce many plants for plant nurseries (**1**)

   (c) Correct order (top to bottom in the table): 3, 4, 1, 2 – all correct for **2 marks**; two correct for **1 mark**

2 (a) Obtain human (stem) cells (**1**) and grow in liquid containing nutrients (**1**).

   (b) Two from: cell culture is quicker (**1**); cell culture is cheaper (**1**); no/fewer ethical objections (**1**); cultured human cells could be used (**1**)

43. Insect-resistant plants

1 (a) Bt comes from the name of the bacterium (*Bacillus thuringiensis*) (**1**); toxins are poisonous substances (**1**)

   (b) (i) Their genome contains the Bt gene. (**1**)

      (ii) **1 mark** for each correct row:

Feature	Disadvantage (✓)
Less chemical insecticide is needed.	
Seeds for GM plants are more expensive.	✓
Insects may become resistant to the BT toxin.	✓
Crop damage is reduced which increases yields.	
The Bt gene might transfer to wild plants by pollination.	✓

      (iii) One from: less chemical insecticide is needed (**1**); crop damage is reduced / yields increased (**1**)

2 (a) The weed plants die but the wheat plants do not. (**1**)

   (b) crop yields increased (**1**) because weeds do not compete for water/nutrients/space/ light (**1**)

   (c) The company's profits could increase (**1**) because they can sell more weedkiller/ glyphosate/seeds (**1**).

44. Meeting population needs

1 use of artificial fertilisers (**1**); use of biological control (**1**)

2 (a) The population of aphids increases slowly at first (**1**) and then very rapidly (**1**), reaching 30 aphids per leaf after 10 days (**1**).

   (b) When ladybirds are present, the number of aphids increases more slowly / does not rise so quickly / is less than without the ladybirds (**1**) because ladybirds eat aphids (**1**) but cannot eat them all / some aphids still survive to breed (**1**).

3 Two from: biological control takes time to act as control agents reproduce (**1**); control agents might become pests (**1**); less pesticide is needed when used with biological control (**1**); chemical pesticides get rid of the pest completely (**1**).

4 One advantage from: contain nutrients/minerals/ions needed for plants to grow well (**1**); increase crop yields (**1**).

One disadvantage from: can pollute waterways (**1**); can cause eutrophication (**1**); expensive (**1**); can reduce soil biodiversity (**1**)

45. Extended response – Genetic modification

*Answer could include the following points:

- Selective breeding produces plants with desirable features.
- Genetic engineering produces plants with desirable features.
- Selective breeding takes many generations but genetic engineering is much quicker.
- Selective breeding has happened for many years but genetic engineering is a recent process.
- Desirable features include resistance to drought/pesticides/herbicides/insects.
- Tissue culture is used to produce clones of a plant.
- Tissue culture does not change plants (unlike selective breeding and genetic engineering).
- Tissue culture allows many plants with desirable features to be produced.
- Some people have ethical objections to genetic engineering / GM plants.
- Selective breeding is widely accepted / people usually do not have ethical objections to it.

46. Health and disease

1 (a) being free from disease and eating and sleeping well (**1**)

(b) how you feel about yourself (**1**)

(c) how well you get on with other people (**1**)

2 (a) Communicable: ✓influenza, ✓tuberculosis; ✓*Chlamydia*; Non-communicable: ✓lung cancer, ✓coronary heart disease

(**3 marks** for 5 correct, **2 marks** for 3 or 4 correct, **1 mark** for 1 or 2 correct)

(b) Communicable: rapid variation in number of cases over time / cases localised (**1**); non-communicable: number of cases changes gradually / cases more widespread (**1**)

3 (HIV) causes damage to the immune system (**1**); reduced immune response / immunity (**1**)

4 (a) Three from: a virus infects a body cell (**1**) and takes over the body cell's DNA (**1**) causing the cell to make toxins (**1**) or damages the cell when new viruses are released (**1**).

(b) Bacteria can release toxins (**1**) and can invade and destroy body cells (**1**).

47. Common infections

1 (a) Zimbabwe (**1**); 15.1–14.3 = 0.8% decrease (**1**)

(b) All countries show a decrease in the percentage of 15 to 49 year olds with HIV (**1**); one example of such a trend is: all percentages have dropped somewhere between 0.3 and 2.9% (**1**).

2 (a) D (**1**)

(b) Two from: leaf loss (**1**); bark damage (**1**); dieback of top of tree (**1**)

3

Disease	Type of pathogen	Signs of infection
cholera	**bacterium**	watery faeces
tuberculosis	bacterium	persistent cough – may cough up blood
malaria	**protist**	**fever, weakness, chills and sweating**
HIV	**virus**	mild flu-like symptoms at first

(all correct for **3 marks**, 3 correct for **2 marks**, 2 or 1 correct for **1 mark**)

4 (a) bacterium (**1**)

(b) Two from: inflammation in stomach (**1**); bleeding in stomach (**1**); stomach pain (**1**)

48. How pathogens spread

1 C (**1**)

2

Disease	Pathogen	Ways to reduce or prevent its spread
Ebola haemorrhagic fever	**virus (1)**	Keep infected people isolated; wear full protective clothing while working with infected people or dead bodies.
tuberculosis	bacterium	**Ventilate buildings to reduce chance of breathing in bacteria / diagnose promptly and give antibiotics to kill bacteria / isolate infected people. (1)**

3 Boil water before drinking / wash hands after using toilet (**1**) because bacteria are spread in water / by touch (**1**).

4 (a) The bacteria are spread in water (**1**); in developed countries water is treated to kill pathogens / good hygiene prevents their spread (**1**).

(b) To prevent being infected by the Ebola virus (**1**) because Ebola virus is present in body fluids of infected people even after death (**1**).

49. STIs

1 an infection spread by sexual activity (**1**)

2 B (**1**)

3

Mechanism of transmission	Precautions to reduce or prevent STI
unprotected sex with an infected partner	using condoms during sexual intercourse (**1**)
sharing needles with an infected person (1)	supplying intravenous drug abusers with sterile needles
infection from blood products	**screening blood transfusions (1)**

4 (a) Viral genetic material inserts itself into the cell's genetic material (**1**) and is replicated with the cell's genetic material (**1**).

(b) because HIV can spend many years in the lysogenic cycle (**1**) and AIDS develops only when HIV enters the lytic cycle (**1**)

50. Human defences

1 (a) Skin acts as a physical barrier that stops microorganisms getting into the body (**1**).

(b) Hydrochloric acid in the stomach kills pathogens (**1**).

(c) (i) lysozyme (**1**)

(ii) kills bacteria (**1**) by digesting their cell walls (**1**)

2 (a) (i) mucus (**1**)

(ii) sticky so traps bacteria / pathogens (**1**)

(b) (i) cilia (**1**)

(ii) The cilia on the surface of these cells move in a wave-like motion (**1**) and this moves mucus and trapped pathogens out of lungs (**1**) towards the back of the throat where it is swallowed (**1**).

(c) Mucus travels down into the lungs carrying pathogens (**1**) because the cilia cannot move and take the pathogens back up to the throat (**1**).

51. The immune system

1 lymphocytes (**1**)

2 Pathogens have substances called antigens (**1**) on their surface. White blood cells called lymphocytes (**1**) are activated if they have antibodies (**1**) that fit these substances. These cells then divide many times to produce clones / identical cells (**1**). They produce large amounts of antibodies that stick to the antigens / destroy the pathogen (**1**).

3 (a) Lymphocytes producing antibodies against measles virus are activated (**1**); these lymphocytes divide many times (**1**), so concentration of antibodies increases (**1**) then decreases when the viruses have all been destroyed (**1**).

(b) Some of the lymphocytes stay in the blood as memory lymphocytes (**1**); these respond / divide after infection (**1**), so the number of lymphocytes producing the antibodies against the measles virus increases rapidly (**1**).

(c) (i) (The girl had not been exposed to the chickenpox virus before because) line B is similar in size and shape to line A (**1**), which was for a first infection with measles / the line would be higher if it was a second infection (**1**).

(ii) The concentration of antibodies increased faster / to a higher concentration (**1**), so the measles viruses were destroyed before they could cause illness / symptoms / disease (**1**).

52. Immunisation

1 (a) A vaccine contains antigens from a pathogen (**1**) that are inactive / unable to cause disease (**1**).

(b) The vaccine causes memory lymphocytes to be produced (**1**), so if the person is exposed to the disease the memory lymphocytes produce a secondary response (**1**); this prevents an increase in the pathogen to a level that causes illness (**1**).

(c) Two suitable such as: mild swelling (**1**); soreness (**1**); a mild form of the disease (**1**); rare major harmful reaction (**1**)

2 (a) 2003 (**1**)

(b) The number of cases would increase (**1**) because fewer babies were immunised which would protect them from infection (**1**).

(c) More babies would become immune (**1**) so unvaccinated babies would be less likely to catch measles / herd immunity (**1**).

53. Treating infections

1 (a) C (**1**)

(b) Antibiotics kill bacteria / inhibit their cell processes (**1**) but do not affect human cells (**1**).

2 The pharmacist's advice would be not to take the penicillin (**1**). The man's cold is due to a virus, so the penicillin will not be effective in combating the infection (**1**).

3 (a) Sinusitis is (probably) not caused by a bacterial infection (**1**).

(b) Same number of patients got better (after 14 days) without antibiotics (**1**), although the patients taking antibiotics may have got better (a little) more quickly (**1**).

54. Aseptic techniques

1 The workbench is wiped with disinfectant before starting work. – So that microorganisms on the bench do not contaminate the culture. (**1**); Petri dish lid is not completely sealed. – To discourage the growth of anaerobic bacteria which are likely to be pathogens. (**1**); In school and college laboratories, cultures are incubated at 25 °C, not 37 °C. – Pathogenic bacteria are more likely to grow at higher temperatures. (**1**); The inoculating loop is sterilised before use. – To prevent cross-contamination between cultures. (**1**)

2 (a) This will stop the entry of any microorganisms from the air (**1**) that are unwanted / not part of the experiment / likely to contaminate the Petri dish (**1**).

(b) This sterilises the loop (**1**) to prevent unwanted microorganisms getting cultured (**1**).

(c) This stops other microorganisms getting in (**1**) and contaminating the culture (**1**).

3 Three from: heating the jelly to 80 °C kills any bacteria or other microorganisms in the jelly (**1**); cooling to 21 °C reduces the risk of harmful bacteria being present in the culture (**1**); warming to a higher temperature produces a more rapid growth (**1**); using sterilised Petri dishes prevents potentially harmful bacteria contaminating the bacterial culture (**1**)

55. Investigating microbial cultures

1 (a) Bacteria do not grow in clear area (**1**) because the antibiotic kills them / stops them growing (**1**).

(b)

Antibiotic	Diameter of clear area (mm)	Cross-sectional area (mm²)
1	7	38.5
2	**11**	**95.0**
3	**12**	**113.1**
4	**10**	**78.5**

1 mark for each diameter and area

(c) disc 3 (**1**); killed the largest area of bacteria (**1**)

2 (a) Use different concentrations of antibiotic (**1**) but the same volume of each (**1**). Repeat with several identical plates and calculate the mean diameter for each concentration (**1**).

(b) Two from: discs are the same size (**1**); same volume of antibiotic solution used (**1**); discs left on the dish for the same length of time (**1**)

56. New medicines

1 (a) 3, 1, 5, 2, 4 (all correct = **2 marks**, 3 correct = **1 mark**)

(b) (i) testing in cells or tissues to see if the medicine can enter cells and have the desired effect (**1**); testing on animals to see how it works in a whole body / has no harmful side effects (**1**)

(ii) by testing in a small number of healthy people (**1**)

(c) Medicine is tested on people with the disease that it will be used to treat (**1**) so that the correct dose can be worked out (**1**) and to check for side effects in different people (**1**).

2 (a) Large number of subjects make the data valid (**1**) and repeatable (**1**); OR side effects will be seen only in small numbers (**1**) so it is easier to notice with a large trial group (**1**); OR there are different stages of the trial (**1**) and each step needs a different group of people (**1**).

(b) The medicine appears to be effective in nearly 400 people with high blood pressure (**1**); this reduction is much greater than those in the placebo group (**1**). You could also say: the medicine seems to have very little adverse effect on the blood pressure of those in the 'normal' group (so it is effective).

57. Non-communicable diseases

1 An infectious disease is caused by a pathogen (**1**) and is passed from one person to another (**1**). A non-communicable disease is not passed from one person to another (**1**).

2 Three from: inherited / genetic factors (**1**); age (**1**); sex (**1**); ethnic group (**1**); lifestyle (e.g. diet, exercise, alcohol, smoking) (**1**); environmental factors (**1**)

3 (a) (i) Bangladeshi men (**1**)

(ii) black women (**1**)

(b) Four from: the prevalence of CHD increases with age (**1**); overall the prevalence is higher in men than in women (**1**), but prevalence is similar in black men and women (**1**); Bangladeshi men have the highest prevalence but Bangladeshi women are in the middle (**1**); ethnic group seems to be a bigger factor in men than in women (**1**); the prevalence in all ethnic groups is very similar in the 40–49 age group (**1**)

58. Alcohol and smoking

1 (a) Ethanol is a drug that is toxic / poisonous to cells (**1**). It is broken down by the liver and harms liver cells (**1**). Too much alcohol over a long period causes cirrhosis / liver disease (**1**).

(b) because it is caused by how we choose to live (**1**)

2 Two from: because carbon monoxide in cigarette smoke (**1**) reduces how much oxygen the blood can carry to the baby (**1**), leading to low birth weight in babies / other abnormalities (**1**)

3 (a) Two from: cardiovascular disease (**1**); lung cancer (**1**); respiratory / lung disease (**1**)

(b) Substances in cigarette smoke cause blood vessels to narrow (**1**) which increases the blood pressure (**1**) leading to cardiovascular disease (**1**).

59. Malnutrition and obesity

1 (a) too little of one or some nutrients in the diet (**1**)

(b) Four from: Anaemia increases with increasing age (**1**) in both men and women (**1**), but whereas there is an increase in females from 1–16 and 17–49 (**1**) followed by a decline (**1**), in males the lowest age groups are 17–49 and 50–64 (**1**).

2

Subject	Weight (kg)	Height (m)	BMI
person A	80	1.80	24.7
person B	90	1.65	**33.1**
person C	95	2.00	**23.8**

All 3 correct = **2 marks**, 2 correct = **1 mark**

3 (a) A = 0.975 ÷ 1.02 = 0.96 (**1**), B = 0.914 ÷ 1.06 = 0.86 (**1**), 1 mark for 2 decimal places for both.

(b) Man A (**1**) because his waist:hip ratio is greater than 0.90 (**1**)

60. Cardiovascular disease

1 (a) Two from: lifestyle changes (1); medication (1); surgery (1)

(b) Two from: give up smoking (1); take more exercise (1); eat a healthier diet (lower fat, sugar and salt) (1); lose weight (1)

(c) because cardiovascular disease reduces life expectancy (1) and can be fatal before treatment can be given (1)

2 Lifestyle changes – Benefits: may reduce chances of getting other health conditions / the cheapest option. Drawbacks: may not work effectively.

Medication – Benefits: starts working immediately / cheaper and less risky than surgery. Drawbacks: needs to be taken long term / may not work well with other medication the person is taking.

Surgery – Benefits: usually a long-term solution. Drawbacks: there is a risk the person will not recover after the operation / expensive / more difficult to do than giving medication.

(3 marks for 6 correct, 2 marks for 4–5 correct, 1 mark for 2–3 correct)

3 Surgery can help prevent heart attacks / strokes (1), but costs more than inserting a stent (1) and surgery has more risk (e.g. risk of infection) (1). However, it can be a long-term solution / other suitable conclusion (1).

61. Plant defences

1 (a) Two from: bark (1); thick waxy cuticles (1); spikes / thorns (1); cellulose cell walls (1)

(b) One from: produce poisons to kill pests / pathogens (1); produce chemicals to stop infection (1)

(c) the control (1)

(d) to stop other bacteria from getting in (1); to stop organisms entering that would kill the bacteria (1)

(e) Two from: temperature (1); same volume of garlic juice and water (1); same species of bacteria (1); same number of bacteria (1); same amount of jelly in each tube (1)

(f) The plant is able to defend itself from attack by pathogens (1).

2 (a) Two from: toxic chemicals (1); bitter tasting chemicals (1); spines on leaves to deter feeding (1)

(b) to kill pathogens (1) to treat symptoms / inflammation (1)

62. Extended response – Health and disease

* Answer could include the following points:
- Antibiotics kill bacteria or inhibit their cell processes and stop them growing.
- Antibiotics can be given after a person is infected with a pathogen.
- Antibiotics are not effective against viruses.
- Bacteria can become resistant to antibiotics.
- Antibiotics can have side effects.
- Vaccines trigger the body's own immune system.
- Vaccines must be given before a person becomes infected.

- Vaccines can protect against viruses as well as bacteria.
- Herd immunity means not everyone needs to be vaccinated.
- In rare cases a person may react badly to the vaccine.

63. Photosynthesis

1 Plants or algae are photosynthetic organisms / producers (1) so they are the main producers of biomass (1) and animals have to eat plants / algae (1).

2 (a) carbon dioxide + water (1) → glucose + oxygen (1)

(b) The product of photosynthesis / glucose has more energy than the reactants (1) because energy is transferred from the surroundings / light (1).

3 (a) Light is required for photosynthesis (1) because only parts of the leaf exposed to light produced starch (1).

(b) Chlorophyll / chloroplasts are required for photosynthesis (1) because only green areas / areas with chlorophyll or chloroplasts produced starch (1).

64. Limiting factors

1 This is a factor or variable that stops the rate of something increasing/changing (1). The rate will only increase if this factor is increased (1).

2 (a) temperature (1)

(b) Add algal balls to hydrogen carbonate solution (1). Leave in light for a set amount of time, e.g. 2 hours (1). Compare the colour change against standard colours (1).

3 (a) Increasing the carbon dioxide concentration increases the rate of photosynthesis (1).

(b) Adding carbon dioxide means that it will no longer be a limiting factor (1), so the plants can make more sugars needed for growth (1).

(c) You could the increase the temperature (1) as this would make photosynthesis happen faster / more quickly (1).

65. Light intensity

1 (a) points plotted accurately (1); curve of best fit drawn (1)

(b) 76 (± 2) (1)

(c) As the distance increases, the rate of bubbling decreases (1), not a linear relationship (1).

(d) (i) Take care not to touch the bulb if it is hot (1).

(ii) Place a water tank next to the bulb if it is hot (1) to help prevent heat from the lamp reaching the test tube (1). OR Use a ruler to make sure that the lamp is at the measured distance (1) because differences in distance will change the light intensity (1).

(e) You could use the light meter to measure the light intensity (1) at each distance and then plot a graph of rate of bubbling against light intensity (1).

66. Specialised plant cells

1 (a) phloem (1)

(b) A There are holes (1) to let liquids flow from one cell to the next (1).

B There is a small amount of cytoplasm (1) so there is more space for the central channel (1).

(c) Mitochondria supply energy (1) for active transport (of sucrose) (1).

2 (a) xylem (1)

(b) Three from: the walls are strengthened with lignin rings to prevent them from collapsing (1); no cytoplasm means that there is more space for water (1); pits in the walls allow water and mineral ions to move out (1); no end walls means that they form a long tube so water flows easily (1)

67. Transpiration

1 (a) Transpiration is the loss of water (1) by evaporation from the leaf surface (1).

(b) stomata (in the leaf) (1)

(c) (i) moves faster (1) because a faster rate of water loss from leaves (1)

(ii) moves more slowly (1); stomata covered so a lower rate of water loss (1)

2 (a) Guard cells take in water by osmosis (1) so they swell, causing the stoma to open (1); when the guard cells lose water they become flaccid / lose rigidity and the stoma closes (1).

(b) The stomata are open during the day, so water is lost by transpiration (1) faster than it can be absorbed by the roots (1). Water is lost from the vacuoles and the plant wilts. At night, the stomata close so water is replaced (1).

68. Translocation

1 (a) the movement of sucrose around a plant (1)

(b) A (1)

2 (a) Radioactive carbon dioxide is supplied to the leaf of a plant (1). The radioactive carbon / sucrose will then be detected in the phloem (1) and eventually incorporated into starch in the potato (1).

(b) Translocation will stop / sucrose will not be transported from the leaf / radioactivity will not be detected elsewhere in the plant (1) because translocation uses active transport (1).

3

Structure or mechanism	Transport of water	Transport of sucrose
xylem	X	
phloem		X
pulled by evaporation from the leaf	X	
requires energy		X
transported up and down the plant		X

(1 mark for each correct row)

69. Leaf adaptations

1 (a) (i) guard cell(s) **(1)**

(ii) Guard cells open stomata during the day and close at night **(1)**; this allows CO_2 to enter during the day and reduces water loss at night **(1)**.

(b) (i) It is thin / transparent **(1)** to allow more light to pass through **(1)**.

(ii) contain a lot of chloroplasts / packed closely together / cylindrical shape **(1)** to maximise locations where photosynthesis can occur **(1)**

(c) Internal air space increases surface area **(1)** to increase rate of diffusion of gases **(1)**.

2 (a) Large leaves also have a large surface area **(1)** so they can absorb more light for photosynthesis **(1)**.

(b) Xylem vessels bring water to the leaf **(1)**; phloem transports sugar away from the leaf **(1)**.

70. Water uptake in plants

1 **One mark** for each correct row:

Information	Increased light intensity	Increased temperature
stomata become more closed		
stomata become more open	✓	
water molecules have less energy		
water molecules have more energy		✓
rate of evaporation increased	✓	✓
rate of evaporation decreased		

2 (a) The rate of evaporation was higher when the fan was on **(1)**, because the movement of air removes water more quickly from the leaves **(1)**, increasing the concentration gradient from leaf to air **(1)**.

(b) The rate of evaporation became quicker than the rate at which the plant could take up water **(1)**; the stomata of the plant closed **(1)** to prevent evaporation from occurring / conserve water **(1)**.

(c) The volume of the tube is calculated using $\pi r^2 l$. volume = $(\pi \times 0.25^2 \times 90)$ = 17.67 mm^3 **(1)**
rate = 17.67 / 5 = 3.5 mm^3 / min **(1)**

71. Plant adaptations

1 (a) Roses produce flowers to attract insects. These flowers have very bright colours/ petals **(1)**, and they also give off a strong scent/smell **(1)**.

(b) They have a light, feathery structure **(1)**, so they can easily be blown away / distributed by the wind **(1)**.

2 large leaves **(1)** to take in as much light as possible **(1)** OR drip tips on the leaves **(1)** to allow water to run off **(1)**

3 (a) Rate of evaporation of water from leaves is reduced **(1)** because leaves have small surface area to volume ratio **(1)**.

(b) (i) waxy cuticle is waterproof **(1)**; less water lost through upper surface of leaf **(1)**

(ii) deep pits and hairs trap water vapour **(1)**; so rate of diffusion of water out of leaf is lower **(1)**

72. Plant hormones

1 (a) X on tip of shoot **(1)**

(b) Y on area just behind the tip on the left-hand side **(1)**

(c) Z on the vertical part of the root **(1)**

2 (a) Phototropism causes shoots to bend towards the light **(1)**. This means that the leaves are positioned better to capture more sunlight for photosynthesis **(1)**.

(b) It causes plant roots to grow downwards **(1)** where there is more water / helps to anchor the plant into the ground **(1)**.

3 (a) The root will grow downwards **(1)**; because roots grow in the direction of the force of gravity **(1)**.

(b) plant roots grow downwards where there is more water **(1)**; helps to anchor the plant into the ground **(1)**

(c) auxin accumulates on the lower surface of the root **(1)**; it inhibits elongation of the cells here **(1)**; so the upper surface of the root becomes longer, making the root bend downwards **(1)**

73. Extended response – Plant structures and functions

*Answer could include the following points:

- Stomata allow carbon dioxide from air to enter the leaf and oxygen to leave.
- Internal air spaces increase the area for diffusion of gases.
- Xylem cells bring water needed for photosynthesis.
- All of these adaptations can increase water loss.
- Water loss is greatest at high temperature / light intensity and dry / windy conditions.
- Plants growing in dry conditions are adapted to reduce water loss.
- Waxy cuticle and stomata sunk in pits reduce water loss.
- Rolled leaves reduce air movements around the stomata.
- Leaf hairs trap moist air around the stomata.

74. Hormones

1 (a) Hormones are produced by endocrine glands **(1)** and are released into the blood **(1)**. They travel round the body until they reach their target organ **(1)**, which responds by releasing another chemical substance **(1)**.

(b) Hormones have long-lived effects; nerves have short-term effects **(1)**. Nerve impulses act quickly; hormones take longer **(1)**.

2 A = hypothalamus **(1)**, B = pituitary **(1)**, C = thyroid **(1)**, D = pancreas **(1)**, E = adrenal **(1)**, F = testis **(1)** and G = ovary **(1)**

3

Hormone	Produced in	Site of action
thyroxine	thyroid gland	various organs including the heart
FSH and LH	**pituitary gland (1)**	ovaries
insulin and glucagon	**pancreas (1)**	liver, muscle and adipose (fatty) tissue
adrenalin	**adrenal gland (1)**	various organs, e.g. heart, liver, skin
progesterone	**ovaries (1)**	uterus
testosterone	**testis (1)**	male reproductive organs

75. The menstrual cycle

1 Two from: oestrogen **(1)**; progesterone **(1)**; FSH **(1)**; LH **(1)**

2 (a) A = menstruation **(1)**; B = ovulation **(1)**

(b) any time between day 14 and about day 17 **(1)**

(c) The lining of the uterus breaks down **(1)** and is lost in a bleed or period **(1)**.

3 (a) Pills, implants or injections release hormones that prevent ovulation **(1)**, and thicken mucus at the cervix **(1)**, preventing sperm **(1)** from passing.

(b) (i) These figures are maximum values **(1)** when the methods are used correctly **(1)**.

(ii) **One mark** for each correct row:

Method of contraception	Reduces chance of pregnancy (✓)	Protects against STIs (✓)
hormonal pill or implant	✓	
male condom	✓	✓
diaphragm or cap	✓	

76. Homeostasis

1 maintaining conditions inside the body at a more or less constant level **(1)** in response to internal and external changes **(1)**

2 (a) the hypothalamus **(1)**

(b) Enzymes have an optimum temperature **(1)** so the body temperature must be kept at this level **(1)**.

(c) Shivering means that energy is released from respiration **(1)** which increases the core body temperature **(1)**.

3 (a) to control the amount of water in the body **(1)** by controlling how much water is lost in the urine **(1)**

(b) to stop the body cells from swelling up **(1)** by absorbing water by osmosis **(1)**

4 The cells would get water/swell/burst **(1)** because cytoplasm is more concentrated than water **(1)**.

77. Blood glucose regulation

1 3, 5, 1, 4, 2. (All 5 correct = **3 marks**, 3 correct = **2 marks**, 1 correct = **1 mark**.)

2 (a) $((7.0 - 4.6) \div 4.6) °— 100$ **(1)** = 52% **(1)**

   (b) Liver / muscle cells take up glucose **(1)** because high blood glucose causes pancreas to release insulin **(1)**.

   (c) Glucose is being taken up by muscles more rapidly **(1)** because they use more glucose during exercise **(1)**.

78. Diabetes

1 (a) As the BMI increases the percentage of people with diabetes increases **(1)** so there is a positive correlation **(1)**.

   (b) (i) BMI = $88 \div 1.8^2$ = 27.2 **(1)**; he (is overweight so) has an increased risk of Type 2 diabetes **(1)** but not the highest risk **(1)**.

      (ii) W:H ratio = $104 \div 102$ = 1.02 which is obese **(1)** so he has a high risk of developing Type 2 diabetes **(1)** because there is a correlation between W:H ratio and risk of Type 2 diabetes **(1)**.

2 (a) Controlling diets will help to control the number of people who are obese **(1)**. Fewer obese people means fewer people with diabetes **(1)**.

   (b) (i) In Type 1 diabetes no insulin is produced so has to be replaced with injections **(1)** but in Type 2 diabetes organs don't respond to insulin **(1)**.

      (ii) A large meal means a higher blood glucose concentration **(1)** so more insulin is needed to reduce the glucose concentration **(1)**.

79. The urinary system

1 (a) A kidney; B renal artery; C renal vein; D ureter; E bladder; F urethra (5 or 6 correct = **3 marks**; 3 or 4 correct = **2 marks**; 1 or 2 correct = **1 mark**)

   (b) (i) urea **(1)**

      (ii) liver cells **(1)**

   (c) A: removes excess amounts of some substances / urea and makes urine **(1)**; B: carries blood from body to kidneys **(1)**; D: carries urine from kidneys to the bladder **(1)**; muscle: keeps exit from the bladder closed until urination **(1)**

2 (a) (i) Proteins stay in the blood **(1)** because they are too large to pass into the nephron **(1)**.

      (ii) Glucose is small so it passes into the nephron **(1)** but is reabsorbed by active transport in the first convoluted tubule **(1)**.

      (iii) Urea is small so it passes into the nephron **(1)** but is not reabsorbed **(1)**; its concentration in urine is higher because water is reabsorbed **(1)**.

   (b) The kidneys help maintain the balance of water and mineral salts **(1)** so sometimes more or less is left in the urine **(1)**.

80. Kidney treatments

1 (a) Waste substances increase in concentration in the blood **(1)** and if not removed the person's life would be in danger **(1)**.

   (b) It separates blood from dialysis fluid **(1)** and allows small molecules to diffuse into the fluid **(1)**.

   (c) same **(1)**, same **(1)**, B higher **(1)**, A higher **(1)**

   (d) This maintains a concentration gradient across the partially permeable membrane **(1)** so urea continues to diffuse out of the blood **(1)**.

2 The concentration in the blood would fall **(1)** because the concentration in the dialysis fluid would be lower so glucose would diffuse into fluid **(1)**.

3 (a) A kidney is removed from a donor and put into the patient's body **(1)** and attached to their blood system **(1)**.

   (b) Patient may have rare antigens / difficult to find donor with matching antigens **(1)**.

81. Extended response – Control and coordination

*Answer could include the following points:

- Cause of Type 1 diabetes: immune system has damaged insulin-secreting cells in pancreas, so no insulin produced.
- Cause of Type 2 diabetes: insulin-releasing cells may produce less insulin and target organs are resistant / less sensitive to insulin.
- Link risk of Type 2 diabetes with obesity / BMI / waist : hip ratio.
- Treat Type 1 diabetes by injecting insulin. Amount of insulin injected can be changed according to the blood glucose concentration.
- Treat Type 2 diabetes by diet (eating healthily and reduced sugar) and exercise.
- Treat more severe Type 2 diabetes with medicines to reduce the amount of glucose the liver releases or to make target organs more sensitive to insulin.

82. Exchanging materials

1 (a) kidneys / nephrons **(1)** to maintain constant water level / osmoregulation **(1)**

   (b) kidneys / nephrons **(1)**; urea is a toxic waste product **(1)**

2 in the lungs **(1)**; oxygen is needed for respiration **(1)**; carbon dioxide is a waste product **(1)**

3 (a) The surface of the small intestine is covered with villi **(1)**. These help by increasing the surface area available for absorption **(1)**.

   (b) This makes the absorption of food molecules more efficient / effective **(1)** by reducing the distance that the molecules have to diffuse **(1)**.

4 Four from: The flatworm is very flat and thin **(1)** which means that it has a large surface area : volume ratio **(1)**; the earthworm is cylindrical so has smaller surface area : volume ratio **(1)**; every cell in the flatworm is close to the surface **(1)**; in the earthworm diffusion has to happen over too great a distance / through too many layers of cells **(1)**.

83. Alveoli

1 (a) Oxygen diffuses from the air in alveoli into the blood in capillaries **(1)**. Carbon dioxide diffuses from the blood into the air **(1)**.

   (b) Millions of alveoli create a large surface area for the diffusion of gases **(1)**. Each alveolus is closely associated with a capillary **(1)**. Their walls are one cell thick **(1)**. This minimises the diffusion distance **(1)**.

2 Maintains concentration gradient **(1)** which maximises the rate of diffusion **(1)**.

3 Three from: breathlessness / shortness of breath / similar **(1)**; less oxygen in blood than normal **(1)** so less respiration / energy **(1)**; increased carbon dioxide concentration reduces pH **(1)** which affects enzyme-controlled reactions **(1)**

84. Rate of diffusion

1 (a) increase in surface area **(1)**; shorter diffusion distance **(1)**; maintenance of a high concentration gradient **(1)**

   (b) surface area: alveoli in lungs **(1)**; diffusion distance: surfaces one cell thick **(1)**; concentration gradient: ventilation of lungs / efficient blood supply **(1)**

2 (a) rate of diffusion would decrease **(1)** by about 3 times **(1)**

   (b) tiredness / fatigue **(1)**; because less oxygen for respiration **(1)**

   (c) Reduced blood flow would reduce the concentration gradient in the lungs **(1)** and so less oxygen would be absorbed for use in respiration **(1)**.

85. Blood

1 plasma - carries other blood components **(1)**; platelet - involved in forming blood clots **(1)**; red blood cell - carries oxygen **(1)**; white blood cell - part of the body's immune system **(1)**

2 (a) nucleus **(1)**

   (b) haemoglobin **(1)**

   (c) Their biconcave shape gives them a large surface area **(1)** for diffusion to happen efficiently. They are also flexible, which lets them fit through narrow blood vessels/capillaries **(1)**.

3 urea **(1)**; carbon dioxide **(1)**

4 Platelets respond to a wound by triggering the clotting process **(1)**; the clot blocks the wound **(1)** and prevents pathogens from entering **(1)**.

5 (a) Infections are caused by pathogens **(1)**; lymphocytes produce antibodies **(1)** that stick to pathogens and destroy them **(1)**.

   (b) Phagocytes surround foreign cells **(1)** and digest them **(1)**.

86. Blood vessels

1 (a) An artery has thick walls **(1)**. These walls are composed of two types of fibres: connective tissue **(1)** and elastic fibres **(1)**.

   (b) Wall stretches as blood pressure rises / heart ventricles contract **(1)** and recoils

Answers

(**not contracts!**) when blood pressure falls / heart ventricles relax (**1**).

2 (a) Thin walls / only one-cell thick (**1**) run close to almost every cell (**1**).

(b) faster diffusion of substances (**1**) because short distance / large surface area (**1**)

3 (a) (i) Blood flows at low pressure (**1**) so no need for elastic wall of arteries / need wide tube in veins (**1**).

(ii) Muscles contract and press on veins (**1**); blood pushed towards heart because valves prevent flow the wrong way (**1**).

(b) Veins have a thinner muscle wall than arteries (**1**) so it is easier to get the needle in (**1**). OR Veins contain blood under lower pressure (**1**) so taking blood is more controlled (**1**).

87. The heart

1

	Carries blood:	
Blood vessel	**from**	**to**
aorta	heart	body
pulmonary artery	**heart**	**lungs**
pulmonary vein	**lungs**	**heart**
vena cava	**body**	**heart**

1 mark per correct line

2 (a) because it acts as a pump (**1**) and muscles contract to pump the blood (**1**)

(b) order of parts: (vena cava) right atrium, right ventricle, pulmonary artery (lungs), pulmonary vein, left atrium, left ventricle (aorta) (names all correct for **2 marks**, 4 correct for **1 mark; additional mark** for correct order)

3 (a) right ventricle (**1**); pumps blood to the lungs / pulmonary artery (**1**)

(b) heart valve closes when ventricle contracts (**1**); prevents backflow (**1**)

(c) has to pump harder (**1**) to get blood all round body (**1**), not just to lungs (**1**)

88. Aerobic respiration

1 (a) oxygen and glucose (**2**)

(b) Diffusion is the movement of substances from high to low concentration (**1**).

2 (a) mitochondria (**1**)

(b) Respiration is an exothermic process (**1**) and transfers energy by heating (**1**).

(c) active transport / muscle contraction / other appropriate use (**1**)

3 (a) glucose + oxygen → carbon dioxide + water (**1**)

(b) capillaries (**1**)

4 (a) Respiration releases energy (**1**) so that metabolic processes that keep the organism alive can continue (**1**).

(b) Two from: Plants cannot use energy from sunlight directly for metabolic processes (**1**) so they need energy from respiration for this purpose (**1**) during the day as well as at night (**1**).

89. Anaerobic respiration

1 (a) Aerobic respiration releases more energy (**1**) per molecule of glucose (**1**).

(b) The body needs energy more quickly than aerobic respiration can supply (**1**); it cannot get enough oxygen to respiring cells (**1**).

2 (a) Heart rates will increase gradually / remain low during early laps (**1**) and increase rapidly during final sprint (**1**) because energy demand is low at first then increases significantly (**1**). You could also say that adrenalin might increase heart rate during early laps.

(b) Two from: to keep heart rate relatively high (**1**) so that lactic acid is removed from muscles (**1**); because oxygen is needed to release energy needed to get rid of lactic acid (**1**)

3 (a) Three from: oxygen consumption increases during exercise (**1**) but reaches a maximum value (**1**); no more oxygen can be delivered for aerobic respiration (**1**); increased energy needed comes from anaerobic respiration (**1**)

(b) During exercise there is an increase in the concentration of lactic acid (**1**); after exercise, extra oxygen is needed to break down lactic acid (**1**).

90. Rate of respiration

1 (a) maintains a constant temperature (**1**); because temperature can affect enzymes / change the rate of reaction (**1**)

(b) Absorbs carbon dioxide produced by the seeds (**1**) so that this doesn't interfere with the movement of the blob of water (**1**).

(c) allows the pressure to be released between experiments (**1**); so the blob of water is pushed back to the start position (**1**)

2 (a) Movement of the blob of water indicates uptake of oxygen for use in respiration (**1**), so measuring the movement of the blob at intervals (**1**) allows the rate of respiration to be calculated by dividing distance moved by time taken (**1**).

(b) Use the water bath at a range of temperatures (**1**); measure distance moved by the blob over a particular time (**1**) and repeat several times at each temperature (**1**).

91. Changes in heart rate

1 (a) Stroke volume is the volume of blood pumped from the heart in one beat (**1**).

(b) (i) cardiac output = stroke volume × heart rate = 75×60 (**1**) = 4500 (**1**) cm^3 / min (**1**)

(ii) Cardiac output increases (**1**); then two from: cells need to respire faster / need more oxygen and glucose (**1**); increased stroke volume / more blood needed for respiring cells (**1**), so heart rate must increase (**1**).

2 (a) $100 - 80 = 20$ (**1**); $20 / 80 \times 100 = 25\%$ (**1**)

(b) highest demand for oxygen / glucose / respiration (**1**)

(c) Rearrange the equation to give stroke volume = cardiac output / heart rate (**1**) = 4000 / 50 = 80 (**1**) cm^3.

92. Extended response – Exchange

*Answer could include the following points:
Outline of route:
● vena cava → right atrium → right ventricle → pulmonary artery → (capillaries in) lungs → pulmonary vein → left atrium → left ventricle → aorta → rest of the body / capillaries in the body → vena cava
Answer might also include:
● valves in heart / veins prevent backflow of blood
● deoxygenated blood enters / leaves right side
● oxygenated blood enters / leaves left side
● walls of left side of heart are thicker than right side.

93. Ecosystems and abiotic factors

1 **1 mark** for each

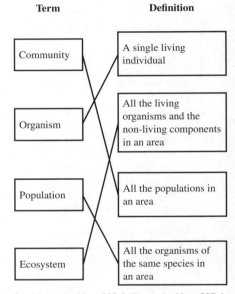

2 (a) south side = 323.5 (**1**); north side = 227.6 (**1**)

(b) She is correct (**1**) because the mean percentage cover is 39% on the south side compared with 4% on the north side / 10 times greater (**1**).

(c) temperature (**1**) because it affects enzymes / rate of reactions (**1**) OR humidity (**1**) because water required for photosynthesis / other cell processes (**1**)

94. Biotic factors

1 (a) the living parts of an ecosystem (**1**)

(b) Two from: so that they can become the new alpha male (**1**); to gain fighting skills (**1**); to become stronger (**1**)

(c) Food can often be scarce in their habitat (**1**), so large groups need to split into different areas in order to find enough food (**1**).

2 The peacock has large, attractive tail feathers (**1**); it competes with other males for mates (**1**), so large showy tails are more attractive to female peahens (**1**). You could also suggest that the large tail feathers can be used to help scare away other male peacocks who may compete for females.

3 (a) The trees emerge through the canopy to get more light (**1**) for more photosynthesis (**1**).

(b) The trees have deep / extensive roots (**1**) to collect minerals (**1**).

95. Parasitism and mutualism

1 both (**1**), parasitism only (**1**), mutualism only (**1**)

2 Cleaner fish get food by eating parasites from the skin of sharks (**1**). This helps the shark because it reduces the risk of the shark being harmed by the parasites (**1**).

3 scabies mite lives in the host and causes it harm (**1**); no benefit to the host (**1**)

96. Fieldwork techniques

1 (a) He could use a 1 m × 1 m quadrat (**1**), which he could throw at the flower bed to choose a random location (**1**).

(b) Using the same area means that his experiment is a fair test (**1**).

(c) He could look at more than one area each day (**1**) and take an average number of slugs (**1**).

2 (a) Find the total number of plants counted and the number of quadrats (**1**) and calculate a mean number of clover plants (**1**).

(b) total size of field = 100 × 65 = 6500 m^2 (**1**), so number of clover plants = 6500 × 7 (**1**) = 45 500 (**1**)

3 Place quadrats at regular intervals along the transect (**1**) and measure the percentage cover of broad-leaved plants in each quadrat (**1**). Record a named abiotic factor (light intensity / temperature) at each quadrat position (**1**).

97. Organisms and their environment

1 (a) Draw a line from the seashore up the beach (at right angles to the sea line) (**1**); place quadrat at regular intervals along the line (**1**); count the limpets in each quadrat area (**1**).

(b) (10 + 8 + 9) / 3 (**1**) = 9 (**1**)

(c) The number of limpets goes down as you travel further from the sea (**1**); this decrease is linear with the distance / it drops by 4 limpets for every 0.5 m distance travelled (**1**); limpets are more likely to survive if they live nearer the seashore (**1**).

2 (a) Instead of placing a quadrat every 2 m, the scientist could place a quadrat every 0.5 m / 1 m / smaller distance (**1**) and use a smaller (**1**) quadrat than before.

(b) Two from: the number of bluebells increases to a maximum around 8 m into the wood (**1**); less light is available for photosynthesis (**1**) and fewer nutrients / water available deeper in the wood where there are more trees (**1**)

98. Energy transfer between trophic levels

1 (a) grass (**1**)

(b) 4 (**1**)

(c) Because there is not enough biomass in the top level (**1**) to provide the energy needed by another level (**1**).

2 (a)

Organism	Energy at each trophic level (J)	Number of organisms	Mass of each organism (kg)	Biomass at each trophic level (kg)
Producers	7550	10 000	0.25	2500
Herbivores	640	200	2.5	**500**
Carnivores	53	10	20	**200**

(**1 mark** for all correct answers)

(b) correctly shaped pyramid with producers at bottom, then herbivores, then carnivores (**1**); horizontal width is drawn to scale (**1**)

(c) (53 ÷ 640) × 100 (**1**) = 8.3% (**1**)

(d) Some of the energy from respiration (**1**) is transferred as heat to the environment (**1**).

99. Human effects on ecosystems

1 Advantage – reduces fishing of wild fish (**1**)

Disadvantage – one of: the waste can pollute the local area changing conditions so that some local species die out (**1**); diseases from the farmed fish (e.g. lice) can spread to wild fish and kill them (**1**).

2 Advantage – may provide food for native species (**1**); OR may increase biodiversity (**1**)

Disadvantage – one of: may reproduce rapidly as they have no natural predators in the new area (**1**); may out-compete native species for food or other resources (**1**)

3 (a) 145 − 15 = 130; (130 / 15) × 100 (**1**) = 867% (**1**)

(b) increasing population (**1**); more food / crops needed (**1**)

(c) Excess fertiliser can be leached / washed into rivers / lakes (**1**), causing eutrophication (**1**).

100. Biodiversity

1 (a) replanting forests where they have been destroyed (**1**)

(b) Two from: restores habitat for endangered species (**1**); reduces carbon dioxide concentration in the air (as trees photosynthesise) (**1**); reduces the effects of soil erosion (**1**); reduces range of temperature variation (**1**)

2 Some species are valuable to humans (**1**) because they are a source of new drugs / are wild varieties of crop plants / source of genes (**1**).

3 The numbers of trees will increase because there are fewer deer to eat them (**1**). This means that there will be more food for birds / bears / rabbits / insects (**1**). There will be more rabbits because there are fewer coyotes to kill / eat them (**1**). If there are more rabbits, there will be more food for coyotes / hawks / predators (**1**). More trees also mean that there will be more habitats for birds / less soil erosion (**1**).

101. Food security

1 (a) access to a reliable **and** adequate food supply (**1**)

(b) Greater numbers mean more food is needed (**1**); as people become better off there is greater demand for meat and fish (**1**).

(c) being able to take what you need to live now (**1**) without damaging the supply of resources in the future (**1**)

2 (a) It would reduce the amount of land for growing food crops (**1**) and so food would become more expensive / poor people could not afford to buy food (**1**).

(b) Two from: growing crops for biodiesel would need use of more fertilisers / pesticides (**1**) or might increase pollution (**1**); could cause deforestation to create more land for growing crops for biodiesel (**1**); could introduce new pests / diseases (**1**)

3 Three from: 7 kg of grain will feed more people than 1 kg of beef (**1**); more land will be required to grow grain for animal feed (**1**) and this could result in deforestation (**1**); intensive farming creates more pollution (**1**) and could increase spread of pests / diseases (**1**)

102. The carbon cycle

1 (a) photosynthesis (**1**)

(b) respiration (**1**)

(c) combustion (**1**)

(d) decomposition (**1**)

2 Microorganisms are decomposers (**1**); they convert complex carbon-containing molecules into carbon dioxide (by respiration), which is released into the atmosphere (**1**).

3 (a) Fish carry out respiration (**1**); respiration releases carbon dioxide into the water (**1**); plants absorb the carbon dioxide (**1**), which is used in photosynthesis (**1**).

(b) Any three from: if there are not enough fish / snails / aquatic animals in the tank there will not be enough carbon dioxide (**1**), so there is less photosynthesis by plants (**1**), so less oxygen is released for fish / snails / aquatic animals (**1**); less food for animals as fewer plants (**1**); plants and fish / snails / aquatic animals die (**1**)

103. The water cycle

1 (a) Three from: evaporation from land (**1**), sea (**1**) and transpiration from plants (**1**); animal sweat (**1**); animal breath (**1**)

(b) Water vapour condenses to form clouds (**1**); water cools to form precipitation / rain / snow (**1**) that returns the water to Earth (**1**).

2 A lot of water evaporates from a golf course so this will lead to more water in the atmosphere (**1**); water levels fall in the river as water is removed for watering the golf course (**1**) so animals or plants living in the river might die (**1**).

3 Advantage: sea water is made potable / safe to drink (**1**)

Disadvantage: needs a lot of energy / fuel / it is expensive (**1**)

Answers

104. The nitrogen cycle

1 C **(1)**

2 (a) Nitrogen fixation by soil bacteria **(1)**.

(b) Three from: nitrates are absorbed by roots **(1)** by active transport **(1)** because plants need nitrogen for making amino acids / proteins **(1)** but can only take in nitrogen in the form of nitrate / ammonium (ions / salts) **(1)**

(c) Amount of nitrate in soil is reduced **(1)** because bacteria convert nitrates in the soil into nitrogen gas in the air **(1)**.

3 (a) Three from: Plants such as clover have nitrogen-fixing bacteria in their roots **(1)** so they can be grown and ploughed back into the soil **(1)**; where they are decomposed **(1)** to add nitrates **(1)**.

105. Decay

1 (a) The conditions needed are oxygen **(1)**, water / moisture **(1)** and warm temperatures **(1)**.

(b) The sun will increase the temperature in the heap **(1)** and the enzymes will work faster **(1)**.

(c) to increase the rate of decay **(1)** because microorganisms need moisture **(1)**

2 (a) Drying: decomposer microorganisms need water for cellular processes **(1)**. Salting: causes water to move out of bacterial cells by osmosis **(1)** so there is not enough water in the cells for them to grow **(1)**.

(b) Refrigeration: cold temperatures mean that microorganisms grow more slowly **(1)** because enzyme activity is reduced at low temperatures **(1)**. Packing in nitrogen: replaces oxygen **(1)** and microorganisms need oxygen to respire **(1)**.

106. Extended response – Ecosystems and material cycles

* Answer could include the following points:

- Fish farming can reduce biodiversity by introducing just one species.
- Waste and diseases can affect wild populations.
- Introduction of non-native species might lead to competition with native species.
- Reduces fishing of wild fish.
- Fertilisers can cause eutrophication leading to loss of biodiversity in nearby water.
- You could also talk about conservation, reforestation, captive breeding.

107. Timed Test 1

1 (a) to produce a foam (with the oxygen) **(1)**

(b) B **(1)**

(c) Two from: volume of hydrogen peroxide **(1)**; concentration of hydrogen peroxide **(1)**; mass of tissue **(1)**; pH of mixture **(1)**

(d) Liver contains catalase **(1)**, which is denatured/damaged/destroyed by heating **(1)**.

(e) The enzyme's active site **(1)** fits hydrogen peroxide but not starch **(1)**.

2 (a) C **(1)**

(b) (i) 0.9 days **(1)**

(ii) 3.85 billion **(1)**

(c) (communicable because) it is caused by a bacterium/pathogen **(1)**

(d) The number of bacteria decreased / the man felt better / antibiotics kill bacteria **(1)**; antibiotics do not affect viruses **(1)**.

(e) (i) antibiotics inhibit cell processes in bacteria **(1)** but not in the host organism **(1)**

(ii) Two from: some disease bacteria remain **(1)**; these bacteria could reproduce **(1)**; remaining bacteria more likely to be resistant to the antibiotic **(1)**; risk of increasing the number of antibiotic-resistant bacteria **(1)**

3 (a) (i) C **(1)**

(ii) homozygous – both alleles for one gene are the same **(1)**; dominant – characteristic is seen even if only one allele is present **(1)**; allele – different forms of the same gene **(1)**; genotype – all the alleles in an organism **(1)**

(b) (i) So he could repeat the experiments and get similar results each time **(1)** because pure-bred peas produce offspring that are identical to the parent **(1)**.

(ii) The factor for green pods was more powerful than / dominant to the factor for yellow pods **(1)** because none of the offspring had yellow pods **(1)**.

(c) (i) D **(1)**

(ii) (ice-cold) ethanol **(1)**

4 (a) nucleus **(1)**

(b) (i) makes / produces / synthesises proteins / enzymes **(1)**

(ii) Two from: plant cell has vacuole **(1)** / chloroplasts **(1)** / nucleus **(1)** / is much larger **(1)**

(c) actual length = 53 ÷ 500 **(1)** = 0.106 mm **(1)** = 106 μm **(1)**

(d) bacterial cell = electron microscope, plant cell = light microscope **(1)** because light microscope has maximum magnification of approx. ×1500 **(1)**

5 (a) Measure weight and height **(1)** every year / at regular intervals **(1)** and plot the results on the chart **(1)**.

(b) (i) heights plotted correctly ± ½ square **(1)**; weights plotted correctly ± ½ square **(1)**

(ii) Boy A is average / below average height **(1)** but in the upper range for weight / overweight **(1)**; Boy B is above average height **(1)** and average weight / possibly underweight for his height **(1)**.

6 (a) Mapping a person's genome means that doctors know if they have an increased risk of testicular cancer **(1)** so they can be monitored more closely / given earlier treatment **(1)**.

(b) (i) Two from: virus inserts its DNA into chromosomes of host cell / forms a provirus **(1)**, replicates with the host DNA every time the host cell divides **(1)**, can remain dormant for a long time **(1)**.

(ii) Because the (pro)virus remains dormant for a long time **(1)** before becoming active and entering the lytic cycle / causing appearance of warts. **(1)**

(c) Answer could include the following points:
- Immunisation involves giving them a vaccine.
- This will protect against infection with HPV
- so they will be less likely to develop genital warts / cervical cancer
- but they must be immunised before becoming sexually active.
- Perhaps boys should also be immunised.
- Vaccines can have side effects.
- Condoms may not give complete protection against HPV
- but condoms can also protect against other STIs.

7 (a) D **(1)**

(b) (i) synapse **(1)**

(ii) Three from: nerve impulse reaches the axon terminal **(1)**; neurotransmitter substance released into the gap **(1)**; this is detected by the next neurone **(1)** which generates a new impulse **(1)**

(c) (i) It would cause loss of feeling in the hand **(1)** because impulses from sensory receptors would not be passed on **(1)**.

(ii) Damage to the spine would cause paralysis **(1)** as well as loss of feeling **(1)** because motor neurones would also be damaged **(1)**.

8 (a) (i) One from: incubate the plates at 25 ºC **(1)**; don't completely seal the Petri dishes **(1)**

(ii) Two from: sterilise agar before use **(1)**; sterilise Petri dishes before use **(1)**; sterilise / flame inoculating loops **(1)**; seal the lid on the dish with tape **(1)**; make sure all surfaces are clean / disinfected before use **(1)**

(b) (i) A = 2.2 **(1)**; B = 53.6 **(1)**

(ii) Antibiotic A is more effective than antibiotic B **(1)** but neither antibiotic completely kills / prevents growth of bacteria **(1)**.

9 (a) There is a positive correlation between alcohol consumption and risk of liver disease / as alcohol consumption increases risk of liver disease also increases **(1)**; the risk increases much more with alcohol consumption greater than 50 g per day **(1)** because ethanol is poisonous, particularly to liver cells **(1)**.

(b) The risk of liver disease is higher for women than for men at all levels of alcohol consumption **(1)** and the risk increases even more steeply above 40 g per day **(1)**.

(c) A **(1)**

10 (a)

Statement	Mitosis only	Meiosis only	Both mitosis and meiosis
used for growth and replacement of cells	✔		
used for production of gametes		✓	
before the parent cell divides each chromosome is copied			✓
produces genetically identical cells	✓		
halves the chromosome number		✓	

(**1 mark** for each correct tick)

(b) (i) advantage: offspring are genetically different / source of variation that is the basis of natural selection / if the environment changes some individuals may survive (**1**) disadvantage: need to find a mate / requires more time and energy (**1**)

(ii) advantage: offspring are genetically identical to parent so if parent is well adapted to environment offspring will be too / only one parent so no need to find a mate / reproductive cycle is faster (**1**) disadvantage: no variation in the population / if environment changes all may die (**1**)

11 (a) D (**1**)

(b) Offspring shown correctly (**1**)

		Parent 1 gametes	
		X	Y
Parent 2 gametes	X	XX	XY
	X	XX	XY

(c) (i) (parent 1) because XY is male / XX is female (**1**)

(ii) 50% / 1 in 2 / 1:1 / ½ (**1**)

12 *Answer could include the following points:

- Animals / plants with good features are crossed.
- Offspring are selected for good features and crossed with each other.
- Process repeated many times until desired characteristics are produced.
- Examples of reasons for selective breeding: disease resistance / increased yields / ability to cope with difficult conditions / faster growth / better flavour.

114. Timed Test 2

1 (a) (i) thermometer / temperature probe (**1**)

(ii) Two from: heat might be lost before the burning food is placed under the tube (**1**); the food might be held too far away from the tube (**1**); draughts might mean heat was lost / did not heat the water (**1**); heat is absorbed by the test tube as well as the water (**1**)

(iii) energy transferred = 500 × 4.2 × 60.8 (**1**) = 127 680 J = 127.7 kJ (**1**); energy content = 127.7 / 8.3 = 15.4 kJ / g (**1**)

(b) (i) biuret test (**1**)

(ii) pale purple / lilac (**1**)

(c) Two from: because more protein will increase the nutritional value of the rice (**1**); as populations grow the demand for protein increases (**1**); increased protein content will mean more food can be grown in the same amount of land (**1**) or without using more fertiliser / pesticide (**1**)

2 (a) (i) 60–65 beats per minute (**1**)

(ii) 7.30 – 8.00 am (**1**)

(iii) His heart rate increased to a peak of about 80 as he walked uphill (**1**) and then fell again shortly before the main peak as he rested (**1**).

(iv) because his muscles were starting to respire anaerobically (**1**) and so they tired more quickly (**1**)

(v) because extra oxygen is needed to replace oxygen used in the exercise (**1**) and to oxidise lactic acid produced (**1**)

(b) (i) person A = 95 × 52 = 4940 (**1**); person B = 58 × 72 = 4176 (**1**); units = cm^3 per min (**1**)

(ii) person A (**1**) because they had a lower resting heart rate / higher cardiac output / higher stroke volume (**1**)

3 (a) (i) Y = capillary wall (**1**); Z = wall of alveolus (**1**)

(ii) diffusion (**1**)

(iii) carbon dioxide (**1**)

(iv) in red blood cells / bound to haemoglobin (**1**)

(b) 408 × 0.15 = 72 m^2 (**1**)

(c) (i) D (**1**)

(ii) rate of diffusion increased (**1**), so more oxygen is absorbed (for respiration) (**1**)

4 (a) **1 mark** for each correct line.

Hormone	Produced in	Target organ
ADH	**pituitary gland**	**kidney**
adrenalin	adrenal gland	various organs, e.g. heart, liver, skin
glucagon	**pancreas**	**muscle**
oestrogen	ovaries	pituitary gland

(b) (i) The uterus lining breaks down (**1**) and the lining and unfertilised egg is lost in a bleed / period (**1**).

(ii) releases hormones (**1**) that prevent ovulation / thicken mucus at the cervix to prevent sperm passing (**1**)

(iii) protect against sexually transmitted infections (STIs) (**1**)

5 (a) B (**1**)

(b) (i) A parasite harms the host (**1**) but an epiphyte does not (**1**).

(ii) One from: large leaves to absorb as much light as possible (**1**); drip tips on the leaves so water runs off (**1**)

(iii) Two from: waxy cuticle (**1**); stomata sunk in pits to reduce water loss (**1**); leaf hairs to trap moist air around stomata (**1**); rolled leaves to reduce air movement around stomata (**1**).

(c) (i) bacteria are protected by the plant / get food from the plant (**1**)

(ii) the bacteria and plants live together (**1**) in a way that benefits them both (**1**)

6 (a) (i) 160 ÷ 8 (**1**) = 20 (**1**)

(ii) C (**1**)

(b) (i) because insulin controls blood glucose concentration (**1**) and they do not produce insulin (**1**)

(ii) Two from: obesity (**1**); activity level (**1**); ethnic background (**1**); type of diet eaten (**1**)

(c) *Answer could include the following points:

Thermoregulation is controlled by the hypothalamus.

If body temperature rises this is detected by the hypothalamus and leads to the following:

- sweat glands release more sweat onto skin surface to evaporate
- sweat spreads out over the skin and so evaporates more easily
- increased blood flow nearer to the surface of the skin
- more heat transferred to environment so body temperature falls.

If the body temperature falls this is detected by the hypothalamus and leads to the following:

- sweat glands stop producing sweat
- body hairs raised by erector muscles
- shivering generates heat
- less blood flow
- less heat transferred to environment so body temperature rises.

7 (a) (i) Two from: light intensity (**1**); water availability (**1**); mineral ions in the soil (**1**); temperature (**1**)

(ii) Two from: predation / grazing by animals (**1**); competition for light and space (**1**); competition for water and nutrients (**1**)

(b) Use a belt transect (**1**), place quadrats at regular intervals alongside the path (**1**), count the number of each different plant species in each quadrat / calculate the percentage cover of each different plant species (**1**), present the results as a table / graph (**1**).

8 (a) (i) ((5.4 − 5.2) ÷ 5.2) × 100 = +3.8% (**1**); ((5.6 − 5.6) ÷ 5.6) × 100 = 0.0% (**1**); **1 mark** for 1 decimal place

(ii) One from: same shape / same size / same temperature / same time left in the solution (**1**)

(iii) One from: repeat and calculate mean values / use a smaller range of concentrations (near the 0% concentration) / use more concentrations in the same range / use a ±0.01 g balance (**1**)

(iv) The solute concentration of the potato cells must have been 0.5 mol dm^{-3} **(1)** because there was no change in mass / movement of water in or out **(1)**.

(b) Dialysis tubing is partially permeable **(1)** so that urea diffuses out of the blood into the fluid **(1)** but dialysis fluid contains the same concentration of useful substances / glucose / mineral ions **(1)** so diffusion restores the normal concentration of dissolved substances in the blood **(1)**.

9   (a) (i) B **(1)**

(ii) E sieve tube **(1)**; F sieve plate **(1)**

(b) (i) B **(1)**

(ii) mitochondria supply energy **(1)** needed for active transport **(1)**

(c) (i) light intensity / carbon dioxide concentration / amount or mass of chlorophyll **(1)**

(ii) Rate increases because reactions happen faster at high temperatures **(1)** and enzymes work faster **(1)** but it decreases again because high temperatures denature enzymes **(1)**.

10 (a) A **(1)**

(b) $((12 - 2) \div 2) \times 100 = 500\%$ **(1)**

(c) *Answer could include the following points:

Disadvantages of salmon farming: uneaten food can cause pollution; salmon produce waste and this can cause pollution; this can lead to local species dying out; diseases (e.g. sea lice) from the farmed salmon can transfer to wild fish and harm or even kill them.

Advantages of salmon farming: provides employment; reduces fishing of wild fish.

Advantages of mussel farming: no food is added to the water, so no uneaten food to cause pollution; mussels remove waste from the water.

Disadvantages of both: reduces biodiversity; can spoil the landscape.

Your own notes

Your own notes

Your own notes

Your own notes

Your own notes

Your own notes

Your own notes

Published by Pearson Education Limited, 80 Strand, London, WC2R 0RL.
www.pearsonschoolsandfecolleges.co.uk

Copies of official specifications for all Pearson qualifications may be found on the website: qualifications.pearson.com

Text and illustrations © Pearson Education Ltd 2017
Produced, typeset and illustrated by Phoenix Photosetting
Cover illustration by Miriam Sturdee

The rights of Stephen Hoare to be identified as author of this work has been asserted by him in accordance with the Copyright, Designs and Patents Act 1988.

First published 2017

20 19 18 17
10 9 8 7 6 5 4 3 2 1

British Library Cataloguing in Publication Data
A catalogue record for this book is available from the British Library

ISBN 978 1 292 13175 7

Printed in Slovakia by Neografia

Acknowledgements

The authors and publisher would like to thank the following individuals and organisations for permission to reproduce copyright material:

Photographs:
(Key: b-bottom; c-centre; l-left; r-right; t-top)
Science Photo Library Ltd: Biophoto Associates 3, Steve Gschmeissner 6, 15
All other images © Pearson Education

Notes from the publisher
1.
While the publishers have made every attempt to ensure that advice on the qualification and its assessment is accurate, the official specification and associated assessment guidance materials are the only authoritative source of information and should always be referred to for definitive guidance.

Pearson examiners have not contributed to any sections in this resource relevant to examination papers for which they have responsibility.

2.
Pearson has robust editorial processes, including answer and fact checks, to ensure the accuracy of the content in this publication, and every effort is made to ensure this publication is free of errors. We are, however, only human, and occasionally errors do occur. Pearson is not liable for any misunderstandings that arise as a result of errors in this publication, but it is our priority to ensure that the content is accurate. If you spot an error, please do contact us at resourcescorrections@pearson.com so we can make sure it is corrected.